MODx Web Development

Building dynamic web sites with the PHP application
framework and CMS

Antano Solar John

PUBLISHING

BIRMINGHAM - MUMBAI

MODx Web Development

First published: March 2009

Production Reference: 1230309

Published by Packt Publishing Ltd.
32 Lincoln Road
Olton
Birmingham, B27 6PA, UK.

ISBN 978-1-847194-90-9

www.packtpub.com

Cover Image by Nilesh Mohite (nilpreet2000@yahoo.co.in)

Credits

Author

Antano Solar John

Reviewers

Shane Sponagle

Susan Ottwell

Acquisition Editor

Viraj Joshi

Development Editors

Sarah Cullington

Siddharth Mangarole

Technical Editor

Mithun Sehgal

Editorial Team Leader

Abhijeet Deobhakta

Project Coordinator

Leena Purkait

Indexer

Rekha Nair

Proofreader

Chris Smith

Production Coordinator

Aparna Bhagat

Cover Work

Aparna Bhagat

About the Author

Antano Solar is a techie to the core—a tech evangelist who is passionate about using technology to revolutionize the learning experience!

Antano has contributed to the open source community in terms of documentation, code, and support, with a variety of platforms based on languages such as PHP, Perl, Lisp, Python, and Ruby.

He loves to share his tech excitement with fellow techies and non-techies, and does so through publishing papers, books, and delivering seminars at colleges, universities such as the IIT, and corporate tech events.

He has published a paper on enhancing wireless networks in an IEEE Journal. His paper on an engine helping machines understand objectives by meta-modelling, using Neuro Linguistic Programming principles and Deep Structure, is considered a landmark.

An avid hacker, Antano has won two Yahoo hack day awards. He recently won the award for developing a Hybrid Search Engine from scratch in 24 hours that uses Machine Intelligence and Social Intelligence to identify, search, and present the information in the required format.

Professionally, Antano, until recently, has been a Consultant and a Trainer providing IT solutions and sessions on VoIP, Networks and Software Plaforms, and Languages. He is currently the Chief Technology Officer at NuVeda Learning. In his current role, he is responsible for the development and deployment of Learning Management Systems that are being used by large MNCs globally. He also plays the role of a Chief Architect in the research and development of technologies related to the understanding and measuring of Learning. He is excited by the challenges of using complex technologies such as Artificial Intelligence and Natural Language Processing.

Occasionally, when Antano needs to take a "Tech" break, he likes to train and tell stories!

To those who prepared me:

My Mom and Dad—for all the hope, faith, love, and wise counsel.

And to those who made it happen:

The Packt team—especially Leena and Sarah—the reviewers,
and the MODx community for an awesome open source
development platform.

About the Reviewers

Shane Sponagle has over 10 years of experience in developing web-based applications. He is currently a senior partner at S/2M2 Design, and has worked on projects ranging from simple web sites to multi-level data-driven applications. Shane is an active member of the MODx community where he enjoys learning about all the interesting ways people are using MODx. He looks forward to collaborating on future publications.

Susan is a self-taught grandmother of eight. She first became interested in computers, both hardware and programming, more than 40 years ago, but got her first computer only a year before the arrival of her first grandchild. She spent a number of years working both independently and as a shop technician building and repairing PCs, from Connecticut to Miami to Israel, while learning various programming and database languages from x86 assembly to dBase to VB to perl in her spare time. For a time, she taught C++ for an online gaming service's "online university".

Her PHP studies began over eight years ago, and have been conducted solely with the assets garnered from the Internet. She discovered MODx when it was still a set of modifications to Etomite, found that it suited her needs, and when MODx forked into its own CMS/CMF system, decided to stick with it, learn it thoroughly, and contribute what she could.

Susan lives quietly, except for a very loud canary named Winston, in a Negev desert community in Israel, the home of PHP. She divides her time between hiking and photography in the desert hills and canyons, quilt making and knitting, and working with MODx on her iBook g4.

I owe everything I've accomplished in the last 15 years to my father and my first husband for telling me I'd never be able to do it, computers weren't of any use, and it's not for girls anyway. They triggered my stubborn streak, and made me determined to do this in spite of them! Then I am indebted to the giants of teaching: Jeff Duntemann, Tom Swan, and especially Gary Cornell, for all of their wonderful books. Certain web sites have become indispensable, among them *Zend*, *O'Reilly's OnLamp*, and *A List Apart*. And finally, perhaps most importantly, I owe Ryan Thrash, Raymond Irving, and Jason Coward for giving me MODx to play with in the first place, and now the rest of the MODx team, whom I only know by their MODx Forum handles. They're way above my head, but they give me something to work towards.

Table of Contents

Preface

This book teaches you how to use MODx for creating powerful dynamic web sites, even without the knowledge of a programming language as a prerequisite. It leads the reader step by step in a logical pattern to build a complete web site. Each chapter covers certain concepts with simple examples. All the examples if you follow along, aggregate to a self-created web site. Towards the end, it has a chapter dedicated to the serious programmers who would like to extend what they can do with MODx.

This book can also be used as a reference or to relearn the particular concepts that have been discussed in each chapter. It has illustrative examples, wherever necessary, to make sure it is friendly. It has a mix of simple demonstrations and in-depth concepts that will interest both the casual and the serious reader

What this book covers

Chapter 1: In this chapter, you will learn the general concepts of web development, and also learn why MODx as a tool is a good choice to develop your web site.

Chapter 2: In this chapter, you will learn how to set up a working platform for developing web sites with MODx, which includes the installation and configuration of the prerequisites such as Apache, PHP, and MySQL.

Chapter 3: In this chapter, you will learn about documents and containers, and how every page that is displayed gets its content from a document. You will also learn to create, edit, and manipulate documents, and manage their configurations, and we will explain the TinyMCE editor.

Chapter 4: In this chapter, you will learn how to create/add templates. We will also take a look at template variables and document-specific variables, and briefly discuss snippets and chunks.

Chapter 5: In this chapter, you will learn how to modify the site to have a signup form and login form. We will also learn how to enable blogs to be posted only by friends.

Chapter 6: In this chapter, you will learn one very useful snippet called Ditto. You will see how to create aggregation and feeds, and how to create feeds for separate categories. You will also learn about tagging, and how to tag documents and use them in MODx.

Chapter 7: In this chapter, you will learn how to use the snippet [[WayFinder]] to create lists of documents. We will also see the usage of parameters in WayFinder to make list creation flexible.

Chapter 8: In this chapter, you will learn how to use the hundreds of snippets available in detail. You will also learn how to search for the snippets that don't come packaged with MODx and how to use them.

Chapter 9: In this chapter, you will learn how to format the values in template variables. You will also learn how to make conditions based on the values of template variables, and accordingly present a different output either from the HTML in the expression or from a chunk or snippet.

Chapter 10: In this chapter, we will use what we have already learned, to study how certain commonly required functionalities can be implemented. We will learn how to integrate a forum, an image gallery, or forms that can send a mail, create web user profiles, and identify similar posts for blogs.

Chapter 11: In this chapter, you will learn how to create snippets, the different ways of displaying their output, and how to implement them. You will also learn to use the available MODx APIs and why you should use them.

Chapter 12: In this chapter, we will discuss how to make the site optimized for search engines. We will also discuss clean URLs, meta tags, sitemaps, and other tweaks.

Chapter 13: Finally, in this chapter, you will learn about plug-ins and modules including the ones that we will use in our application. The chapter will also cover events and plug-in configuration.

What you need for this book

No knowledge of PHP programming or any templating language is needed, but the more advanced chapters towards the end of the book will allow more confident developers to extend their applications even further by creating their own snippets.

Who this book is for

This book is ideal for those who want to learn to use MODx. Both beginners and experienced web developers will benefit from this comprehensive guide to MODx.

Conventions

In this book, you will find a number of styles of text that distinguish between different kinds of information. Here are some examples of these styles, and an explanation of their meaning.

Code words in text are shown as follows: "You have already seen an example of document-specific template variables when you used [*#content*] in the template that you created in the last section."

A block of code will be set as follows:

```
<div id="menu">
[!Wayfinder?startId=`0` &level=`1`!]
</div>
```

When we wish to draw your attention to a particular part of a code block, the relevant lines or items will be made bold:

```
<div id="menu">
[Wayfinder?startId=`0` &level=`2` &outerClass=`outer`
&innerClass='inner' &lastClass=`last` &firstClass=`first`
&hereClass=`active!]
</div>
```

New terms and **important words** are introduced in a bold-type font. Words that you see on the screen, in menus or dialog boxes for example, appear in our text like this: "Click on the **Manage Resources** menu item from the **Resources** menu."

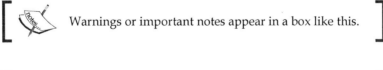

Warnings or important notes appear in a box like this.

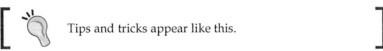

Tips and tricks appear like this.

Reader feedback

Feedback from our readers is always welcome. Let us know what you think about this book, what you liked or may have disliked. Reader feedback is important for us to develop titles that you really get the most out of.

To send us general feedback, simply drop an email to feedback@packtpub.com, making sure to mention the book title in the subject of your message.

If there is a book that you need and would like to see us publish, please send us a note in the **SUGGEST A TITLE** form on www.packtpub.com or email to suggest@packtpub.com.

If there is a topic that you have expertise in and you are interested in either writing or contributing to a book, see our author guide on www.packtpub.com/authors.

Customer support

Now that you are the proud owner of a Packt book, we have a number of things to help you to get the most from your purchase.

Downloading the example code for the book

Visit http://www.packtpub.com/files/code/4909_Code.zip to directly download the example code.

The downloadable files contain instructions on how to use them.

Errata

Although we have taken every care to ensure the accuracy of our contents, mistakes do happen. If you find a mistake in one of our books—maybe a mistake in text or code—we would be grateful if you would report this to us. By doing this you can save other readers from frustration, and help to improve subsequent versions of this book. If you find any errata, report them by visiting http://www.packtpub.com/support, selecting your book, clicking on the **let us know** link, and entering the details of your errata. Once your errata are verified, your submission will be accepted and the errata added to the list of existing errata. Any existing errata can be viewed by selecting your title from http://www.packtpub.com/support.

Piracy

Piracy of copyright material on the Internet is an ongoing problem across all media. At Packt, we take the protection of our copyright and licenses very seriously. If you come across any illegal copies of our works in any form on the Internet, please provide the location address or website name immediately so we can pursue a remedy.

Please contact us at `copyright@packtpub.com` with a link to the suspected pirated material.

We appreciate your help in protecting our authors, and our ability to bring you valuable content.

Questions

You can contact us at `questions@packtpub.com` if you are having a problem with some aspect of the book, and we will do our best to address it.

1
What is MODx?

MODx is a content management system and an application framework. MODx makes it quick and simple to create web sites that are interactive and that can expose different functionalities depending on the kind of user visiting the site. The creation of all this is made possible without the user having any coding background as many of its powerful features work out-of-the-box without any code changes. MODx and its shipped components are modular and well abstracted so that the same components provide multiple behaviors, determined by how they are used.

Content management system

A content management system allows you to do the following:

- Manage content
- Set content management rules
- Define content

Manage content

This means allowing a user to create, publish, edit, and organize content. A good CMS assumes that the user has no technical knowledge. Hence, it provides an easy-to-comprehend user interface for managing content. A flexible CMS will maintain ease of use, even for a novice, and yet give much flexibility to the professional. Publishing the content must extend beyond just displaying the content to designing how the content is shown, making the content accessible and allowing easy search of the content based on various criteria.

Content management rules

These allow the management of content to be delegated and distributed from just one user to many. Different access levels can be granted to different groups and users can belong to any of those defined groups.

Define content

Managing content is fine! But what exactly is content? A good CMS allows the end user to define what content is. Content can be anything! It can be raw text, pictures, videos, music, or a combination of a few, or all, of them. A necessity in any CMS is to allow the user to define types of content and give such types a name.

An application framework

An application framework is an integrated platform that makes the process of developing and maintaining applications a lot simpler. Often they support a certain development methodology and provide interfaces and tools to make the development rapid and agile.

Any application framework serves two primary purposes:

Reusable program components

Any code that has been written once should be available for use within the same application and in other applications. This is called reusability. Generally, high reusability is achieved by careful planning and adherence to an objected-oriented paradigm. An application framework reduces the overheads in making such reusable program components and handles many of the coding overheads internally.

Abstracting logic from presentation

In a simpler sense, separating logic from presentation means separating any programming code from whatever is finally rendered to the end user. Whatever is finally rendered to the end user is generally known as presentation. Ultimately, what a browser can render is generated by the presentation layer and is known as the **Document Object Model (DOM)**. The DOM has structure, presentation, and behavior. Structure is generally defined by HTML, the presentation by CSS, and behavior using JavaScript. Separation of logic from presentation means keeping everything mentioned above, which belongs to the DOM, away from actual code. Application frameworks help in achieving such a separation by providing what is generally known as templating languages. MODx also allows separation of logic from presentation, but how it helps you do this is quite different from what is commonly known as templating among developers.

Web development methodologies

The development of web sites has evolved over the years. They initially originated from just hyperlinked pages that provided a wealth of information, evolving to complex objects being exposed as URLs at runtime. When wanting to develop a site, there are multiple options that one may choose to develop with. A briefing on the most widely known methodologies follows.

Old school—conventional three tiers

This approach is to use a programming language to create a complete site or application from scratch without using any third-party templating system or framework. In this method, there are three layers:

- Client side
- Server side
- Database access

In this architecture, a user requests a page. Every request is processed by executing an appropriate server-side script. A server-side script is any piece of code that gets processed and helps the server send a response to the client. A common example of a server-side language is PHP. Every code that executes in the user's system or the client's system is called client-side script or language. HTML and JavaScript are such client-side languages as they are processed and rendered by the web browser in the user's computer. Whenever needed, any stored information is fetched by the server-side script from the database and any new information is saved in the database. This approach is called the **Three-Tier Architecture**, as generally, the activities of rendering output, processing the script, and manipulating the database are spread across three layers of systems.

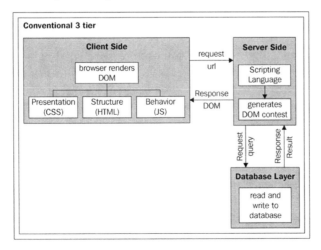

Advantages of the conventional three tiers

One advantage of the conventional three-tier architecture is that it has fewer dependencies. Generally, the only real dependency for such sites is the language itself and the database as well, if used. Hence, they can be run in any environment that supports the language and, if necessary, the database server. This advantage looks minimal considering the other overheads and the increasing support for CMSs and frameworks among the hosting providers.

The only restriction on what you can do is the limitation of the language itself. Coding everything from scratch along with the overheads also brings the flexibility of doing anything exactly the way you want it to function. The only limitation of what can be done and what cannot be done will be what is imposed by the language itself. Again, this is not a real advantage as the emerging technologies are being built so abstract that they impose almost no restriction themselves.

The conventional three-tier architecture can be used to develop new development methodologies. Whatever the framework or the CMS may be, beneath the surface they must all follow the same core rules. Hence, something about these systems takes care of handling requests and generating responses at the lowest layer, which the developer need not worry about. These components that take care of such activities are themselves coded in the conventional three-tier architecture.

Disadvantages of the conventional three tiers

Having to reinvent the wheel is a big disadvantage of the conventional three-tier architecture. Any big project will have a common set of functionalities that are repeated. Many projects have in fact emulated an existing CMS or framework in the process of building their own tools. This is just repetition of work and time that could have been spent in more productive thoughts. Most projects written in the conventional three-tier method end up reinventing the wheel, at least for the concepts of "formatting output" and "database abstraction".

Another disadvantage is that the three-tier architecture is error prone. The language allows you to get things done. It doesn't check if they are cleanly done or not. Hence, it is very simple to write code that gets something done but not so easy to write clean code that gets the same thing done, even in the worst conditions.

The three-tier architecture is also difficult to maintain. It could be said that code is more read than written. And in this approach, since HTML is mixed with server-side code, and appears messy, it is hard to read and maintain such code. Also, if the custom-written libraries are not well documented by the developers who wrote them, then the maintenance becomes even harder as one must read the code to understand its functionalities.

URL mapping becomes complex with the three-tier architecture. It must be noted that in most cases, the job of a server-side script is just to generate client-side output that can be rendered in the browser. So, when such an HTML page with further possible actions is created, the server-side script must be able to generate navigational elements and carefully map the links to a server-side script that can handle the particular request. That is, it has to map a URL to server executable code. This can get tedious to maintain as the site grows, or when a new team is introduced to maintain the code.

Security becomes problematic with the three-tier architecture. The language may have security vulnerabilities like SQL injection. Or there may be security bugs introduced by the programmer. Since in this approach all the functionalities are taken care of by the programmer, there must be strong security testing for every written functionality and different combinations of use-case scenarios. It is also possible that certain situations can go unforeseen. Writing secure code in such an architecture requires strict discipline and is laborious.

Templating

Templating is the idea of using files, which are very similar to regular HTML files, to render output. These template files have what is known as variable replacement, or commands similar to a programming language, called directives, that can be inserted within HTML. Hence, this approach clearly separates what is called presentation from logic. Apart from this single concept, everything else is the same as the approach mentioned above. And it inherits all the advantages and disadvantages from above. The ones in addition to those already mentioned are listed below.

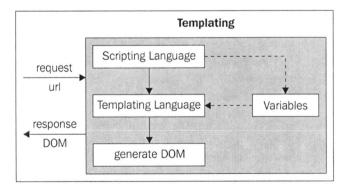

Advantages of templating

One of the advantages of templating is that view is separated from logic, as explained in the previous figure.

Disadvantages of templating

One of the main disadvantages of templating is that there is a small learning curve of a new templating language. Every new templating language introduces a new syntax and, hence, a small learning curve. The time it takes to learn a templating language depends on the complexity of the system. However, a programmer can generally start using a templating language with just the reference or cheat sheets.

Application frameworks

Application frameworks are systems built on top of a programming language to let the developer focus only on the logic of the application. The framework takes care of the other repetitive work. All frameworks at least have the well-known features of "URL Mapping", "DB Abstraction", and "Templating". How each of these is implemented internally is specific to the framework. Every framework also exposes a methodology, the most famous of which is called MVC, which stands for Model, View, and Controller. The framework itself will contain documentations and libraries for frequently used functionalities and, hence, making the developer's work easier. Every framework also tries to ensure cross-browser compatibility, cross-platform support, and many other clean practices, most importantly the RESTful approach. For more information on RESTful practices, read www.xfront.com/REST-Web-Services.html.

Advantages of application frameworks

One of the main advantages of application frameworks is that there is a high reusability of code. Frameworks encourage architectures where higher reusability of code is possible. They also provide enough APIs to do the most common tasks so that you don't have to rewrite them.

They provide clean practices at no extra effort. Most frameworks follow clean practices, and since they allow you to take care only of the logic, the internals are handled by the framework. Hence, while you may not even know it, you have generated applications that adhere to clean practices!

Application frameworks have good testing mechanisms. Generally, application frameworks also provide some kind of helpful mechanisms to make the testing easier. Most MVC frameworks auto-generate test files, or at least a very useful skeleton for each unit of functionality being implemented.

In application frameworks, view is separated from logic, which is similar to using a templating language. Most frameworks allow a mechanism for separating view from logic. Some frameworks do this by using a templating language that the framework understands. But that is only one way of doing it, and many frameworks follow different approaches to achieve the same outcome.

Database abstraction means writing a system in such a way that if you were to only change the database server that stores your data, your system would still work without any necessary code changes. Also, most frameworks have an implementation of the concept called **Object-Relational Mapping (ORM)**, which allows the developer to manipulate the database as objects and provide simpler syntax to achieve complex queries.

Disadvantages of application frameworks

While developing with application frameworks, there is a big learning curve in understanding the development methodology that the framework understands and expects you to follow. Getting used to a new development methodology can take some time.

All application frameworks have framework-specific syntaxes for a lot of functionalities that they expose. It takes some time to be able to get to the exact documentation when you need it.

Most MVC frameworks have a single templating system, or DB abstraction layer, already defined that you have to use. For some applications, this might be a limitation, or maybe you just prefer something else. This is a small disadvantage. Certain frameworks, like "Catalyst", allow one to choose between the individual components as well.

Content management systems

Content management systems are a very interesting idea. The focus of any content management system is that the end user must be able to create web sites that can be self maintained without any programming knowledge. A CMS makes it simple to create the kind of sites that are generally known as **Web 2.0**. Web 2.0 just means sites in which the content being displayed is created by the end users and not the developers of the site. There are numerous content management systems and each has its own exposed architecture. To use a content management system, one must understand the basics of the particular system, and then comprehension and insight on how one does development with that particular system logically fit in. Hence, one can quickly start creating powerful and dynamic web sites.

Advantages of content management systems

While using a content management system, often the only thing that is required to build the site is to let the system know what type of content you want, how you would like it to be displayed, and who can do what! Almost everything else is handled by the system. This allows the developer to focus on the key areas of any web site, which are the content itself and its presentation.

Most of the content management systems come without the prerequisite of needing to know a programming language. Though knowledge of the language helps in many ways, one can still build powerful and custom sites without any prior experience. Moreover, all CMSs are so user friendly with onscreen help and wizards, that you have all that you need to get started right in front of you. Perhaps, simplicity is the keyword for any CMS. Of course, the simplicity mentioned here is what is called pseudo-simplicity, where a complex system hides within itself all of the complexity but exposes a simple usability.

Content management systems come with necessary demonstration templates and sample pages that can be used to quickly kickstart the web site. In most CMSs, almost without any effort, you have the baseline to start with, and all that is left to do is customizing the site to your requirements.

Disadvantages of content management systems

Simple sites are alright. But when the requirement grows, creating everything with what is already available requires a new mindset. Often the biggest hurdle that developers find in getting used to a content management system is that everything is defined as content and not objects or functions. So every component that is available for download speaks in terms of what it does with the content. And often it is required to use multiple components to get what you need. This is the case with any well-abstracted system; it takes a new mindset to learn it!

Many CMSs introduce the requirement of some templating language to be able to customize the look and feel of the site. In such cases, there is an overhead of learning the templating language as well as learning how to use the templating language to create a new look and feel within the CMS used.

A big disadvantage of a CMS is that you are restricted to the functionalities provided by the CMS. Depending on the exposed architecture, there could be practical limitations on the extendibility of the CMS. Certain CMSs cannot be extended much beyond what they already have to offer. Certain CMSs can be extended a little, but not by much more. Some CMSs can be extended, but only at the cost of learning complex APIs and methodologies that are specific to the CMS. There are also certain CMSs that allow extendibility with just the knowledge of the programming language in which they were written.

Why MODx?

As the following image shows, MODx breaks the limitations that are generally around CMSs and yet gives the simplicity necessary to instantly start developing.

Why a CMS?

Content management systems are used when one wants to create a site that can be self-maintained. It really does replace a programmer for maintenance. The web sites for most companies have simple work flows, if any. And there are a lot of individuals who would like to have a web site for themselves, just like everyone wanted to have a business card. Content management systems avoid having to pay professional rates for simple web sites when you can create and maintain such sites yourself. You might want to create the web site with a professional but still maintain it yourself for quicker turnaround time in updating new content. These are situations where a CMS like MODx provides a solution.

Why an application framework?

Application frameworks take over where the limitations of CMSs begin—when you want more than what is possible. To use any application framework, you must know the language it uses. But if you really want to develop, then you better be a programmer, just a smart one who lets the system handle "the obvious things"!

So, why Modx?

MODx gives the ease of a CMS and the extendibility of a framework, which is made possible by exposing a new architecture that is both easy and flexible. It is possible to create very complex and custom sites in MODx. Hence, one can start developing a complete site in MODx without any programming knowledge and use expertise only for the elements that need programming skills if they are needed.

Another interesting concept of MODx is how it handles templating. Unlike most CMSs available, there is no need to learn any templating language to introduce a theme to your site. Hence, it does not even have the small learning curve of a templating language.

MODx is designed to be intuitive; hence, it is easy for anyone to understand how to create sites quickly and effectively. Once you have learned the basics, you will realize that the experience keeps getting better.

MODx administration is AJAX-driven, hence, giving you the ability to manage the site with abilities that are really user friendly. The sites created with MODx can also have AJAX-enabled features without much effort. Many built-in snippets, such as the AJAX search snippet available for MODx, come with interesting AJAX functionalities that can be used out of the box.

MODx is search engine friendly, which means that it has everything to help you get your site listed on Google or any famous search engine.

MODx is an open source project and, like most open source projects, it has strong community support. There are countless places to get help from when you are stuck, and almost all queries get answered within less than a day. Moreover, having community support just means that it will only keep getting better.

All this makes MODx suitable both for a casual developer who would like a quick site and also for serious developers who want something easy to start with and to build sophistication gradually. MODx uses an architecture that helps overcome most of the disadvantages mentioned under application frameworks and CMSs while retaining the advantages.

Overview of the book

This book teaches you how to use MODx for creating powerful dynamic web sites, even without the knowledge of a programming language as a prerequisite. It leads the reader step by step in a logical pattern to build a complete web site. Each chapter covers certain concepts with simple examples. All the examples if you follow along, aggregate to a self-created web site. Towards the end, it has a chapter dedicated to the serious programmers who would like to extend what they can do with MODx.

This book can also be used as a reference or to relearn the particular concepts that have been discussed in each chapter. It has illustrative examples, wherever necessary, to make sure it is friendly. It has a mix of simple demonstrations and in-depth concepts that will interest both the casual and the serious reader.

Summary

In this chapter, you have learned the general concepts of web development and also been assured as to why MODx as a tool is a good choice to develop your web site. The various development methodologies, especially a CMS and a Web Application Framework have been explained. With these briefings on the fundamentals, you must by now have a clear understanding of what MODx is and why would you want to use it.

2
Getting Started

This chapter takes you through setting up and running MODx. It also refers to online documentation resources and discusses how to get community help. It sets the base for developing the example application in this book.

Setting up the development environment

This section of the book will help you to install MODx and verify that it is working.

Prerequisites

The following is the list of software packages that have to be installed for MODx to work. If you have them installed and configured already, you can skip this section. Otherwise, you can read only the instructions that are specific to your operating system.

- PHP
- MySQL
- Apache

MODx is built using PHP, which stands for PHP hypertext processor. PHP is a server side language and we need a web server that can interpret PHP. We are using Apache for this, which is the most widely used web server. Apache is not really a prerequisite, any web server that can interpret PHP would do.

MODx uses MySQL as the database server.

For the sake of simplicity and consistency of settings and configurations, throughout the book we will be using a package called XAMPP that bundles Apache, PHP, MySQL, and tools to get you easily started with a local development environment.

This section will show you how to set up the prerequisites for different OS.

Linux

XAMPP for Linux is available for download from `http://www.apachefriends.org/en/xampp-linux.html#374`.

Download the latest stable release available. You will get a file like `xampp-linux-(version number).tar.gz`.

1. To begin installation, open a shell prompt like konsole or gterm.
2. Change the current directory to the directory where you have downloaded XAMPP. If you have downloaded it to the desktop, type `cd ~/Desktop`.
3. To install XAMPP, you must have super-user rights. If you are not the super user, type "su" followed by the password at the prompt to get root user permissions. Some operating systems like Ubuntu do not have a super user. In such a case, you must prefix "sudo" before the commands mentioned here.
4. Now type `tar xvfz xampp-linux-(version number).tar.gz -C /opt`. If you have done everything properly so far, you will have installed XAMPP successfully.
5. To start the XAMPP server, type `/opt/lampp/lampp start`. If XAMPP has been started successfully, you will see a line like this: "LAMPP started".

[The Linux version of XAMPP was previously called LAMPP and so you may see LAMPP where you expected XAMPP.]

Windows

XAMPP for Windows is available for download at `http://www.apachefriends.org/en/xampp-windows.html`. Download the version that is packaged as a Windows Installer file, as it is easier to set up.

Run the setup file and choose the installation directory. After successful installation, you will see a small icon in the task bar that lists the enabled services. Make sure that Apache and MySQL are running. If they are not, click on the **Start** button next to the Apache and MySQL services. Your Windows firewall might ask if you want to block these services. If asked to do so, click on the **Unblock** button.

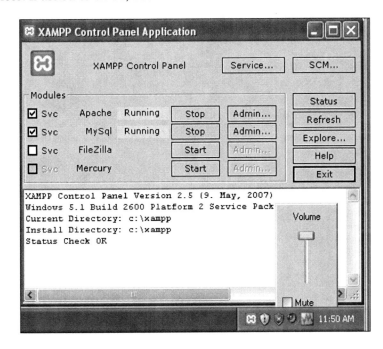

Note that we are using XAMPP here only to make things simpler for you to get started. You can use any web server that supports PHP, including IIS.

MAC

MAMP is the easiest way to get started in a MAC machine. It can be downloaded from http://www.mamp.info/en/mamp.html and installed like any other MAC application.

Verification

To verify that the installation is working, open the browser and type http://localhost. You will see a page similar to the following if everything is installed correctly.

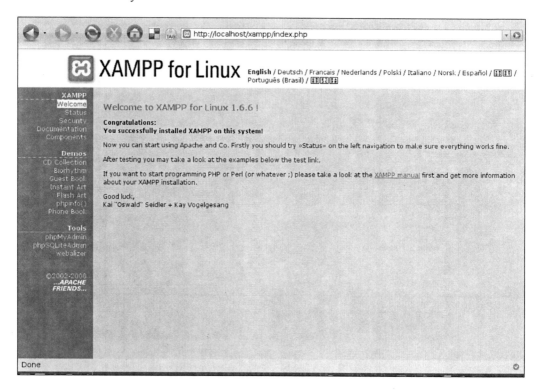

Downloading MODx

MODx is available for download from http://MODxcms.com/downloads.html. MODx is distributed under the GNU General Public License which, on a lighter note, means that you can download it for free, install it on as many sites as you like, and even modify and redistribute it under a new name. For more information about the license, read http://MODxcms.com/license.html.

Like most open source projects, MODx has a stable release and a preview beta release. The stable release is what has been tested and made ready for production. For any production use, you must be using the stable version. The preview and beta release is to test out new features and possibly identify any bug in the process of using it. There is also a development snapshot that can be checked out (downloaded) from the SVN repository (http://MODxcms.com/svn.html) as the developers make changes.

For this book, we will be using the stable version. The stable version at the time of writing was **0.9.6.1p2**. Click on the link that allows you to download the stable version, and unzip it using any ZIP utility your operating system supports like WinZip, WinRAR, or TAR.

Installing MODx

Unzip the downloaded archive and place it in a folder named learningMODx within the root directory of your web server. This should be a directory named www or htdocs under your apache or XAMPP installation.

Possible Root Folders can be one of the following depending on the installation:

- /var/www/
- /opt/xampp/htdocs/
- c:\program files\xampp\htdocs

Now open http://localhost/learningMODx. If everything is fine so far, you should be seeing something like this:

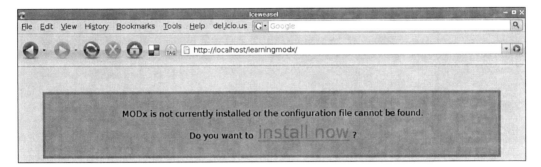

Creating a database

MODx needs one database to store all the data. This database must be created, and the appropriate username and password must be given for a user who has privileges to read and write to the database.

MODx can create the database for you if the MySQL user that you specify in the setup page has permissions to create the specified database.

With the default installation of MODx, there is only one user with the name "root", and it is not a good idea to use this user for MODx or any similar platforms. This is because the database username and password are stored in plain text files and someone with access to just MODx files can bring down all the databases, sometimes even unintentionally.

- There are two methods to get the databases configured: You can create a user and grant that user privileges to create a database. In such a case, MODx can use that user and create the database for you.
- You can create the database and the user yourself.

In this example, we will create both the user and the database. phpMyAdmin comes along with XAMPP and is not related to MODx.

1. In a new browser page, open http://localhost/phpmyadmin.
2. Click on the **Privileges** link and then click on **Add a new user**.
3. In the new user page, for the purpose of this book, create the username as **learningMODx**, give the password as m0dxdbus3r, and make sure you select the option **Create database with same name and grant all privileges** and click **Go**.

Here we have created a user called learningMODx and also a database with the same name, and we have granted all privileges on this database to that user.

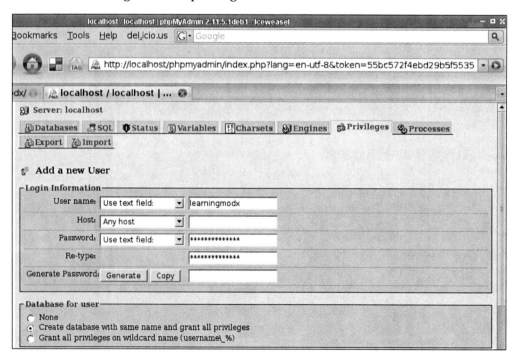

If you are familiar with MySQL, you can also do the same with the following query using your MySQL client.

```
create database learningMODx;
grant usage on *.* to learniningMODx@localhost identified by
                                      'learniningMODx';
grant all privileges on learningMODx.* to learningMODx@localhost ;
```

Starting the installation

The next step is to go to the page where you opened `http://localhost/ learningMODxy` and click on **Install now**.

1. Select the language and click **Next.**

2. Click on **Begin**. You can always change anything that you have chosen in the previous page by clicking on the **Back** button.

3. Read through the agreement. MODx is released under a GNU license. Click on **I agree to the terms set out in this license** and click **Next.**

4. You will be asked about what you want the installer to do. For a site that is not yet installed, a new installation radio box will be the only option enabled. Click on the **Next** button.

5. You will see a page like the following.

Enter this information into the following fields:

- **Database name**: The database that MODx must use. Fill it with the name of the new database that we have created: **learningMODx**.

- **Database Login Name**: Set the value of this field with the username we created: **learningMODx**.

- **Database Password**: Set the value of this field with the password that you gave during creation.

- **Test Connection**: After entering the preceding details, check that the database connectivity is working by clicking on **Test connection**. This will show a small label indicating if the connection succeeded or not.

- **Default Admin User**: MODx allows the user to manage the site from a frontend manager interface without having to look into the code or database. We will call this interface the manager interface. The **Default Admin User** can log in to the manager interface. Fill in the fields with the relevant details for this user and remember the username and password to be able to administer the site. Now proceed with the installation by clicking **Next**.

The next step is to check all the checkboxes in the next page and continue with the installation. These checkboxes tell MODx to install all the available resources and a sample site. It is not necessary in a production environment to check all the options, especially not the demo site. Here we are installing everything so that we can also learn by looking at the existing content once we are familiar with the basics. Each of the resources that you have selected will be explained in detail in the later chapters.

Installation status and diagnostics

The next page makes a check to ensure that everything is working correctly. The only things that can go wrong are permissions on certain folders that have to be writable. In such a case, you will see messages in red describing which folders have to be writable but are not. The folders that require write permission during installation are assets/cache, assests/images, and assests/export. In Windows systems, this can be changed by right-clicking on the respective folders and choosing permissions. In Linux systems, use this command to change permissions:

```
$chmod -R 0666 (foldername)
```

You might also be required to create a file named config.inc.php in the manager/includes/ folder with writable permissions. This file gets written automatically most of the time, but in some server environments that use IIS, it will not be possible to do so. If the web server has write permissions for the folder manager/includes/, then MODx will create config.inc.php automatically. However, this is not a good security practice.

You will then see an **Installation Successul** page with an option to delete the `install` folder. It is a good security practice to always delete that folder after installation. You don't want someone trying to reinstall your site, though he/she may not get very far without knowing your database access details.

After installation with the demo site, visit `http://localhost/learningMODx` and you will see a page like the following:

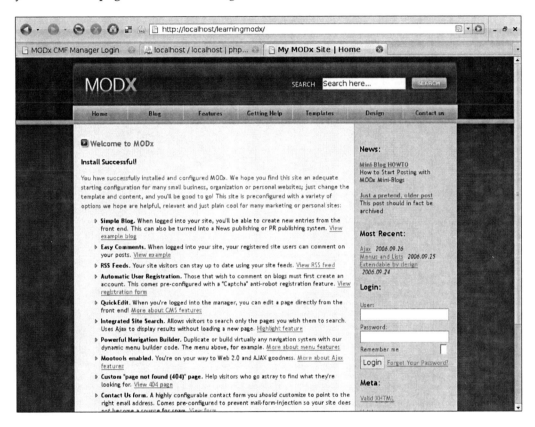

Also make sure that you are able to log in with the default admin user that you created. Open `http://localhost/learningMODx/manager` and type in your default admin username and password. After a successful login, you will see a page similar to the following:

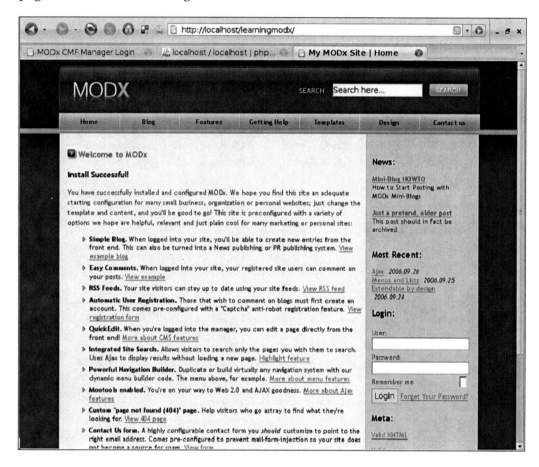

Congratulations! If you have reached this point so far and can see the last page, it means that you have successfully installed MODx with the demo site and are all set to start learning and developing along with the instructions in the book.

Documentation

The most important resource for learning any open source technology is the documentation that it comes bundled with. This section introduces you to the available documentation for MODx.

There are two kinds of documentation available:

- Official documentation
- Community-driven documentation

Official documentation

The official documentation for MODx is available from the official MODx site: `http://MODxcms.com/documentation.html`. The official documentation tries to contain as much text as possible to cover everything about MODx. But due to the rapid level at which changes happen and the process involved in making documentation official, the official documentation does not cover everything. You can be assured that whatever is covered in there is free from error. It can be a very good resource to start with but, as you progress with MODx, you will find that there are other forms of documentation that are more interesting.

Community-driven documentation

Community-driven documentation is those write ups and aggregated knowledge that are shared among MODx users. The MODx wiki and MODx forums contain a wealth of community-driven documents. Though the MODx wiki has not caught up with the pace of the project's progression yet, it still has some useful documentation. You can access the MODx wiki at `http://Wiki.MODxcms.com`. The MODx forum is very active. When you are stuck with any situation and need to know if someone has already cracked it for you, it helps to do a search on the forum first. Many such concepts that have already been cracked are available as small how-tos. For many snippets that you might be using, you will also find a support thread in the forums to make it easier for you to learn more about the snippet and read about what other users have experienced before. The MODx forums can be accessed at `http://MODxcms.com/forums/index.php`.

Getting support

What happens when you are stuck? When you have already searched the forums and have tried googling and still you haven't found a solution to your problem? That's when you can use the community to get interactive support. There are two common mediums of interactive support, the forums and **IRC (Internet Relay Chat)**.

Before we discuss more about forums and IRC, the following is a list of guidelines one must always remember in order to get helpful replies.

- Before asking, thoroughly check if what you are asking has already been answered in the forums.

- Don't ask to ask. That is, do not ask questions like "Can I post a question?"

- Be specific with your questions. Always make sure that when you are asking a question, you explain these three in context:

  ○ What you tried

  ○ What result you expected

  ○ What result you have got instead

- Know your terminology. It is easier to be precise when you know the right terminology to use when asking your question.

- Be patient! Sometimes it may take a while before someone notices your questions and posts an answer.

- Always use a pastebin service when posting large lines of code. There are services that allow you to post code and give you a URL that you can use to share the code with others. One such pastebin service is `www.rafb.net/paste/`. Use such services when posting code to maintain uncluttered continuity of the conversation.

- Capital casing and red coloring are considered to be shouting.

- Ask the question in the related room or thread.

- Remember, a well-formed question is half answered. Your response is directly related to the kind of questions that you ask. There is a tutorial written on how to ask questions the smart way. It can be accessed at `http://catb.org/~esr/faqs/smart-questions.html`. Reading this tutorial really helps a lot for getting any community help.

Web forums

You need to register before you can post queries to the forums. The MODx forum is just like any other forum where you can post your queries and can expect them to be answered. If you cannot find any other suitable threads, then the thread **Support | General Support** is a good place to place your queries.

IRC

Most open source projects have IRC communities supporting the project. MODx has one too. To be able to use the IRC service, you need an IRC client. The most popular IRC client for Windows is **mIRC**, which can be downloaded from http://www.mirc.com/. In Linux, all the famous instant messengers, such as pidgin and kopete, support IRC. IRC has the concept of servers and channels. When you connect to a server, you may join the channels available in that server. MODx has a channel "#MODx" for itself in the server "irc.freenode.org". This channel is only for MODx-specific questions. If you have a question that is related to PHP, it will be answered in #php in the same server.

Summary

In this chapter, you have learned how to set up a working platform for developing web sites with MODx that includes the installation and configuration of the prerequisites like Apache, PHP, and MySQL. To make the process easier, you have used XAMPP, which is a bundle containing all these packages. Finally, you have installed MODx and have verified that everything is set and ready.

3
MODx Basics

In this chapter, you will learn the basics of MODx and how to create a Front Page for the site. The basic elements explained in this chapter are:

- Site configurations
- Documents and containers
- Manager interface
- TinyMCE editor

Site configuration

When you first log in to the MODx Manager interface, you will see the site configuration page on the right panel. Here, you can customize some basic configurations of the site. You can reach this page from anywhere in the MODx Manager by clicking on the **Configuration** sub-menu in the **Tools** menu.

All the options that can be configured from this Configuration page are settings that are global to the entire site. After changing the configurations, you have to let MODx store them by clicking on the **Save** button.

The following is the screnshot of the Configuration page:

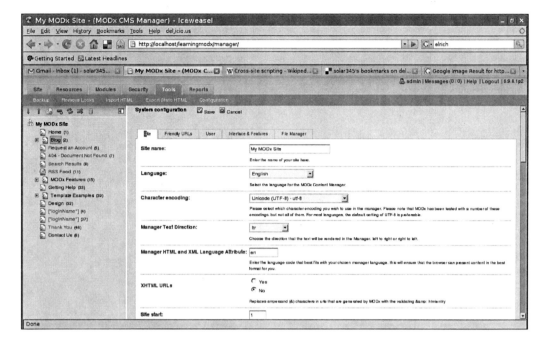

The configurations are grouped into five categories:

- **Site** — mostly, settings that are used to personalize the site
- **Friendly URLs** — settings to help make the site search-engine optimized
- **User** — settings related to user logins
- **Interface & Features** — mostly, Manager interface customizations
- **File Manager** — settings of what can be uploaded and where

Configuring the site

In this section, we are going to make a few changes to get you familiar with the various configurations available. We will learn what some of the other configurations mean as we proceed through the book. Most configurations have tooltips that describe them in a little pop-up when you move the mouse over them.

Default Manager interface page

After making changes in the site configuration and saving it, you will be redirected to another page. This page is available by clicking on the **Home** link on the **Site** tab. This page is also the default Manager interface page. This means that every time you log in using the Manager login screen, you will reach this page by default.

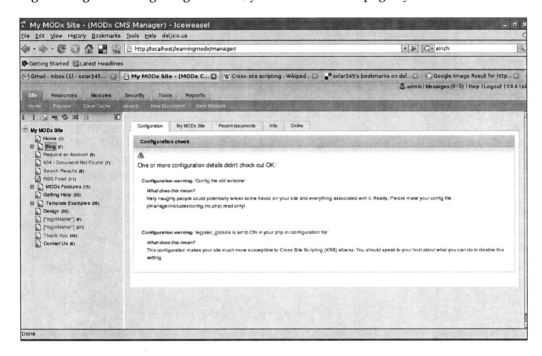

This page has five tabs, which are briefly explained below:

- **Configuration** — displays information on the current status of the site
- **My MODx Site** — provides quick access to certain features in MODx
- **Recent documents** — shows a list with hyperlinks of the recently created/ edited documents
- **Info** — shows information about your login status
- **Online** — shows all the active users

Noticing and fixing errors and warnings

The **Configuration** tab of the default Manager interface page displays errors and warnings about issues in the installation, if any. Generally, it also has instructions on how to fix them. Most times, the warnings are for security reasons and better performance. Hence, though the site will continue to work when there are warnings listed in this page, it is good practice to fix the issues that have caused these warnings.

Here we discuss two such warnings that occur commonly, and also show how to fix them.

- **Config file still writable**: This is shown when the `config` file is still writable. It can be fixed by changing the properties of the configuration file to read only.

- **register_globals is set to ON in your php.ini configuration file**: This is a setting in the PHP configuration file. This should be set to `OFF`. Having it `ON` makes the site more vulnerable to what is known as **cross site scripting (XSS)**.

Changing the name of the site

We have listed the groups of configuration options available in the previous section. Let us change one option—the name of the site—now.

1. Click on the **Tools** menu in the top navigational panel.
2. Click on the **Configuration Menu** item.
3. Change the text field labeled **Site Name** to **Learning MODx**.
4. Click on the **Save** button.

The basic element of MODx: Documents

Documents are the basic building blocks in MODx. They are the elements that make up the content of the site. Every web page in MODx corresponds to a Document page. Every document has a unique ID. This ID can be passed along in the URL, and MODx will display the page from the document with the same ID. As the simplest possibility, a document contains plain text.

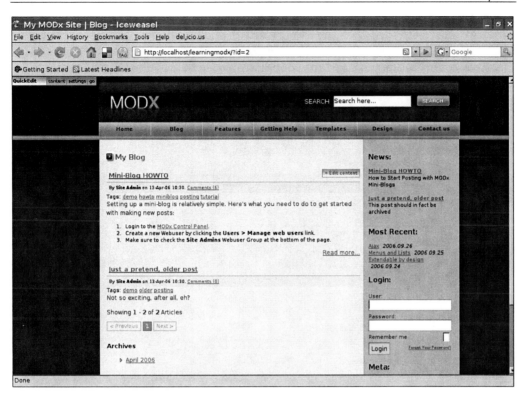

As can be seen from the previous screenshot, the ID referred here is 2, and the content displayed on the screen is from document ID 2. It is also possible to refer to a document by an alias name instead of an ID. An alias is a friendly name that can be used instead of having to use numbers. It will be explained in more detail later in the book.

Containers

Documents can be contained within other documents called containers. Containers in MODx are like folders in filesystems, but with the difference that a container is also a document. This means that every container also has a document ID, and a corresponding page is shown when such an ID is referenced in the URL.

MODx Manager interface

MODx is administered and customized using the provided Manager interface. From the Manager interface, you can edit documents, place them within containers, and change their properties. You can log in to the **Manager** interface using the Manager login screen `http://sitename/manager` with the username and password that you supplied when installing MODx. The Manager interface is divided into two panes. The left pane always displays the documents in a document tree, and the right pane displays the content relevant to your last action.

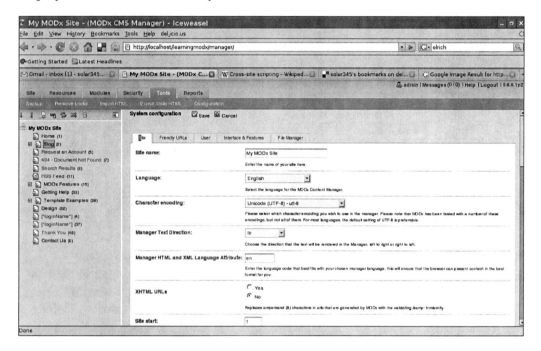

Above, the two panes you see are the menu and the corresponding menu items. Each of these leads to the different functionalities of MODx.

In the left pane, you will see the site name followed by a hierarchically-grouped document list. There is + near every unexpanded container that has other documents. When you click on the + symbol, the container expands to show the children and the + symbol changes to a – symbol. Clicking on the – symbol hides the children of the respective container. The document's ID is displayed in parentheses after the document's title in the document tree.

The top of left pane consists of a few icons, referred to as the Document Toolbar, which help to control the visibility of the document tree.

- **Expand tree**—expand all the containers to show their children and siblings.
- **Collapse tree**—collapse all the containers to hide their children and siblings.
- **New document**—open a new document page in the right pane.
- **New weblink**—open a new weblink page in the right pane.
- **Refresh tree**—refresh the tree of containers and documents to make available any changes that are not yet reflected.
- **Sort the tree**—open a pop-up page where you can select from the various available criteria to sort the tree.
- **Purge**—when you delete a document, it stays in the bin. The documents are stricken out with a red line. The documents can be completely removed from the system by clicking on the purge icon.
- **Hide tree**—this icon slides in the left pane, giving more space for the right pane.

Right-clicking on a document brings up a contextual menu from where you can perform various actions on the document. Clicking on **Edit** will open the page for editing in the right pane. The contextual menu provides interesting shortcuts that are very handy.

Using the HTML editor

MODx is bundled with a **What You See Is What You Get (WYSIWYG)** editor. So, documents can be edited and modified without having to know HTML. This section shows you how to use the editor.

To edit any document, click on the corresponding document from the left pane and click on **Edit**. Scroll down till you see the section with the title **Document Content**. Here, you can edit the document using any installed text editor, or you can edit it as plain HTML. You can toggle this option by selecting the appropriate method from the editor using the drop-down box. With the default installation, you have two choices—**TinyMCE** for a WYSIWYG editor and **None** for editing plain HTML.

This section discusses the TinyMCE editor that we installed during the MODx installation process. TinyMCE is an open source software provided by `http://tinymce.moxiecode.com`.

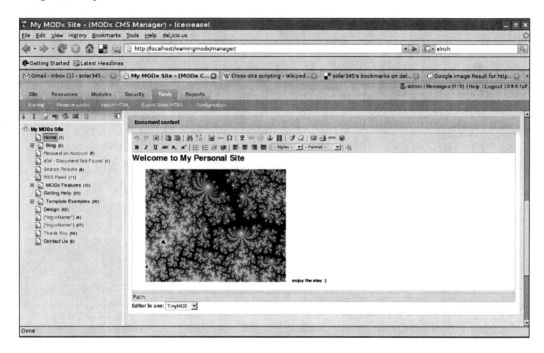

The TinyMCE editor comes with handy tools to make the editing of your documents easier. It has small buttons on the top that you can click to perform the appropriate actions. Moving the mouse cursor over these buttons brings up the tooltip that displays the name of the button and the keyboard shortcut, if any. Using the keyboard shortcut can be handy when you are required to use a button multiple times. The available buttons and many other settings can be changed from the site configuration that was discussed earlier.

Creating the Front Page

Now you should understand what documents are and how the Manager interface allows you to create and control them. We will now create a Front Page.

In the Manager page perform the following steps:

1. Click on the **Document** with ID 1 in the left panel,

2. Click on **Edit** and fill in the following details:

   - **Title: Home**
   - **Long title: Welcome to Learning MODx**
   - **Description: My Personal Site using MODx**
   - **Summary: The welcome page to my visitors**
   - **Uses template: MODxHost**

3. Insert some content that you would like to have in the Front Page, replacing the existing content from the demo site.

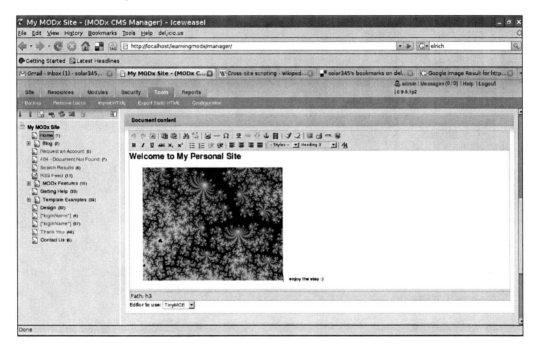

4. Click on **Save**.

5. Click on the **Preview** menu item in the **Site** menu to open a preview of the site in a new window.

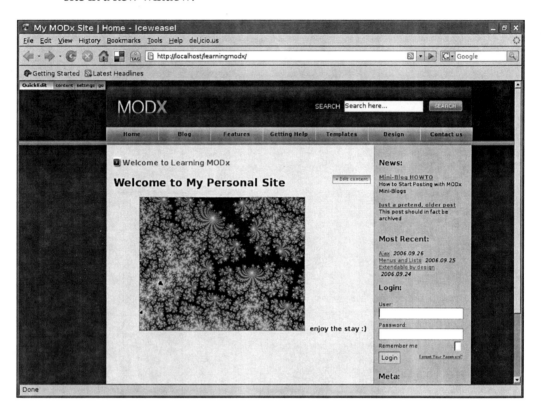

6. Click on the **Configuration** menu item in the **Tools** menu.

7. Change the **Site name** to whatever you want to name your site.

8. Click on **Save**.

You might want to change the entire content of your Home Page instead of just the content area. We will introduce templates in the next chapter, which will allow you to make all your content have a consistent and interesting look.

When editing documents, it is good practice to save them frequently. Since you are editing the documents through the web site, if you take too long before you save, then the page will get timed out, which will result in the loss of any changes that you had made.

QuickEdit module

In the last screenshot, you should notice two buttons: **Edit content** and **QuickEdit**. These two functionalities are available to quickly edit and manage documents and related properties without having to go back to the Manager interface. These functionalities are available when you:

- Log in as an admin in the Manager page, and open a new tab or new window and visit any page in the site
- Click on **Preview Document** from within the Manager interface

When you click on **Edit content**, it opens up the same rich text editor as a pop-up page.

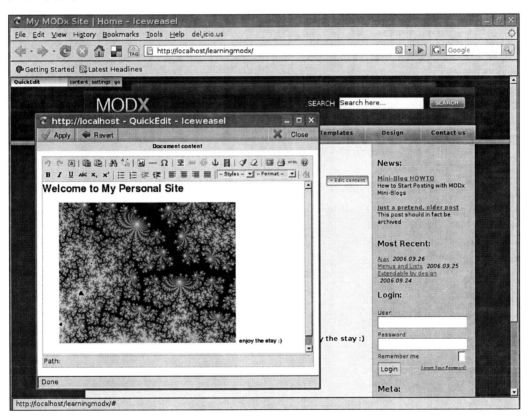

Once you make changes to the content in the pop-up window, you can see the changes in the original page by clicking on the **Update** button. When you are done with editing the content, click on the **Close** button. The **QuickEdit** bar shows a drop-down menu when you click on it, allowing you to change many properties that are discussed next. When you click on **Edit content** in the **QuickEdit** bar, you will see the same pop-up that you saw when you clicked on the **Edit content** link. **Edit content** and the **QuickEdit** bar are not always shown, and what can be edited using the **QuickEdit** bar is configurable. They are discussed in more detail in the following chapters.

Documents revisited

This section gives more information on documents and their properties.

Editing documents

A document has many properties attached to it. Changing their values changes its behavior. When you click on **Edit** after clicking on a document, you will see the following options for the caption after saving.

- **Add another**—creates a new document as you save the current document
- **Continue editing**—remains in the same page even after saving the current document
- **Close**—closes the current page after saving the document

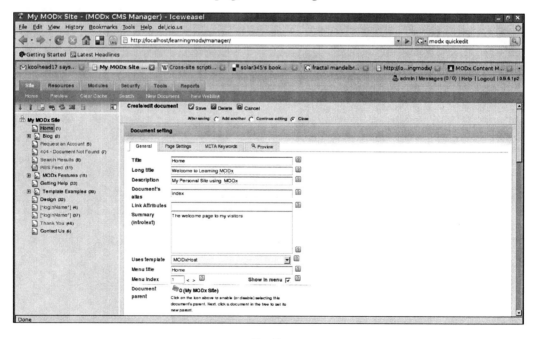

Document properties

The following are the Document properties:

General tab

- **Title** — the title of the document. This is generally a short title that gets displayed when listing your documents.

- **Long title** — the long title of the document. This is a more descriptive title of the document.

- **Description** — here, you can set the optional description of the document.

- **Document's alias** — when friendly URLs are enabled, the documents can be accessed using a friendly name called the alias instead of the ID. Here, you can set the document's alias.

- **Link Attributes** — when this document is opened through a link, you might want it to open in a relative window. Here, you can specify the relative targets for the link.

- **Summary (Introtext)** — a brief summary of the document can be specified here, depending on whether or not your templates use the summary. More of the document properties that are used in the templates are explained in the next chapter.

- **Uses template** — set the template within which the document's content will be used. Templates are explained in detail in the next chapter.

- **Menu title** — Here you can specify the title that you would like to use as a menu item if your document is accessible from a menu. If no menu title is set for the page, the page title will be used by default.

- **Menu index** — Menus can be generated in MODx dynamically. This is explained in detail in the chapter on menus (Chapter 7). **Menu index** allows you to have fine control over the ordering of the menu. For example, menus can be sorted in the ascending or descending order of the menu index. **Menu index** is a number assigned to the document to allow this fine control over dynamically generated menus.

- **Document parent** — documents can be organized to be within containers. A document parent is the container within which you would like this document to be. To select the document parent, click on the small green icon next to this field, and then click on the document that you would like to have as the parent document.

Page Settings

This page provides checkboxes to enable and disable the properties already discussed previously. The list of these checkboxes is:

- **Container**
- **Rich text**
- **Log visits**
- **Published**
- **Searchable**
- **Cacheable**
- **Content Type**

Besides these checkboxes, you also have the following fields:

- **Publish date**: You can use this field to publish the document on a future date. You can select the publishing date by clicking on the *calendar* icon next to this field. You can remove the publishing date by clicking on the icon next to it.
- **Un-publish date**: This is similar to the above field, but it un-publishes the page on the specified date.
- **Empty cache**: If you want MODx to clear the current cache of the document, leave this field checked. Once you save the document properties, the cache is cleared for this document and this field gets unchecked.
- **Content Disposition**: This is a drop-down box with two options:
  - **Inline**: When the document is accessed, its contents are rendered by the browser.
  - **Attachment**: When the document is accessed, its contents are available for download as a file.

Meta Keywords tab

Here, you can add a list of keywords that are saved as the document's Meta Keywords. This is discussed in more detail in the chapter relating to search engine optimization (Chapter 12).

Preview tab

This shows a preview of the current document, and has a link to save and refresh when the old contents of the document are being rendered after editing the document.

Besides the properties in this tab, there are two other sections, which are discussed in detail in the following chapters. These properties are:

- Template variables
- Access permissions

Summary

In this chapter, you have learned about documents and containers and how every page that is displayed gets its content from a document. You have also learned to create, edit, and manipulate documents, and manage their configurations along with the explanation of the TinyMCE editor. The chapter also explained each and every configuration option for documents, and also the general configurable options of the site. Finally, you have created a Front Page using what you have learned and the quick edit module has been introduced.

4
Templating

Templates are the HTML layout within which a requested document's content is displayed. Templates can themselves be dynamic and can have different elements that show different things depending on various factors. The content of a template includes dynamic data, where the same template shows different content depending on the document requested. In this chapter, you will learn about templates and the elements that make dynamic content possible in templates. These are called template variables.

Changing the template of a document

If you have followed along and have created the Front Page from the previous example, your web site will look like this:

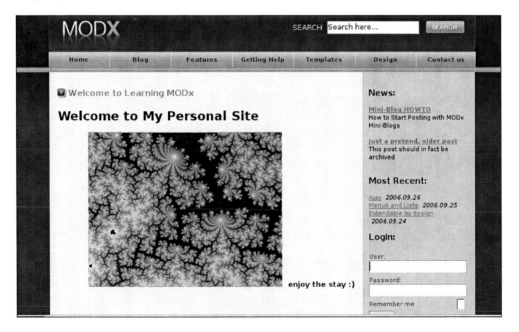

Now, to practically get a feel of what templates are all about, let us go ahead and change the template of the Home Page to None. You will immediately notice that all the menus and layouts have disappeared and only the content of the document is shown. Later in the chapter, we will go on to create our own template.

Follow these steps to modify the template of the Home Page to None:

1. Log in as admin to the Manager Interface.
2. Click on the **Home** document in the Document tree.
3. Click on **Edit** and change the option **Uses template** to **(blank)**. The document editing page will refresh, but the change to the document is not yet saved.
4. It may warn you about losing previous publishing dates. Click on **Yes** to continue.
5. Click on **Save** to save the changes.
6. Click on **Preview** to see how the modified home page looks.

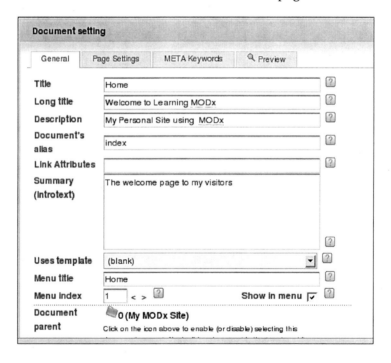

Now the Home Page will look similar to the following:

We have asked MODx to not use a template for the Front Page. Hence, the contents of the document are rendered as such without being embedded within any other HTML structure. Earlier, we used the MODxHost template and the output was quite different.

We are now going to create a template of our own using simple HTML and make our document using this template. This will explain the process of creating the template and also how to mark a portion within the template as the area in which to render the contents of the document.

Creating a new template and giving it a category

To start with, let us create a simple template that has a content area, header, and footer.

The HTML and CSS code for a structure like that is discussed in this section:

HTML

The following HTML creates a header, body, and footer layout. The content div is where the content of a document will be displayed.

```
<!DOCTYPE html PUBLIC "-//W3C//DTD XHTML 1.1//EN" "http://www.w3.org/
TR/xhtml11/DTD/xhtml11.dtd"> <html
  xmlns="http://www.w3.org/1999/xhtml" xml:lang="en">

<head>
<title>Learning MODx</title>
```

```
<meta http-equiv="Content-Type" content="text/html; charset=iso-8859-
                                                                    1" />
<link rel="stylesheet" type="text/css" href="assets/templates/
learningMODx/style.css" />
</head>
<body>
<div id="banner">
<h1>Learning MODx</h1>
</div>
<div id="wrapper">
 <div id="container">
  <div id="content">
   [*#content*] <!-- This is the only line that is not HTML.It is
                           explained in the sections below. -->
  </div>
 </div>
  <div class="clearing"> </div>
</div> <!-- end of wrapper div -->
<div id="footer">It is fun and exciting to build websites with
                                         MODx</div></body>
</html>
```

CSS

The following CSS adds colors, borders, and padding to the preceding HTML layout.

```
* { padding:2; margin:0; border:1; }
body { margin:0 20px; background:#8CEC81; }
#banner { background: #2BB81B; border-top:5px solid #8CEC81; border-
bottom:5px solid #8CEC81; }
#banner h1 { padding:10px; }
#wrapper { background: #8CEC81; }
#container { width: 100%; background: #2BB81B; float: left; }
#content { background: #ffffff; height:600px; padding:10px; }
#footer { background: #2BB81B; border-top:5px solid #8CEC81; border-
bottom:5px solid #8CEC81; }
.clearing { clear:both; height:0; }
```

This book assumes that the reader is already familiar with HTML and CSS. As you will see, MODx makes it possible to use static HTML and CSS to be converted into dynamic templates.

Steps to create the new template

Let us use the just-mentioned HTML to create a new template that we will use, for now, to display our documents:

1. Click on the **Resources Menu** in the top navigation panel from within the Manager interface.

2. Click on the **Manage Resources** submenu.

3. The templates tab is selected by default; if it is not, click on it.

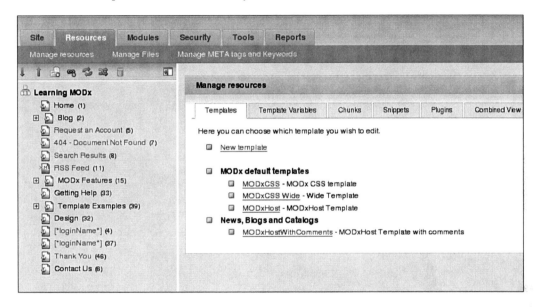

4. Click on **New Template**. You will see a screen like the following:

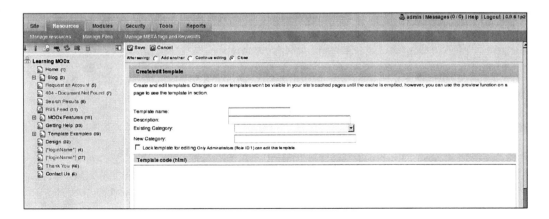

The following is an explanation of the various fields:

- **Template name** — name of the template to be created.
- **Description** — a friendly description to help you remember when you come back to your code later.
- **Existing Category** — one or more templates and other resources in MODx can be grouped together for personal organization. It will make it easier to remember which template to edit when you have a lot of them. From this drop-down, you can use an already existing category.
- **New Category** — the same concept as the above field. When you enter a value in this field, a new category is created and the template is assigned to that category.

> Description and Category are there to just help you remember and group the templates when you want to use or edit them later. Their values don't affect any output of the site.

For the sake of this example, insert the following values into the aforementioned fields.

Name	Value
Template name	Learning MODx default template
Description	The default template to use for the whole site
Existing Category	[There will not be any values here yet]
New Category	Learning mod x
Template Code	Type in the HTML given in the *HTML* section

Now click on **Save** to create the new template. Since our template uses an external CSS file, we need to create a file called `style.css` and save it with the CSS content given in the *CSS* section.

As you can see from the HTML code, we are using this CSS file for our template.

We can save the CSS file anywhere but it is always good to stick to conventions and store it in the `assets/templates/templatename` folder, within the root of the MODx installation. In our example the root of the MODx installation is the `htdocs/learningMODx` folder. We will henceforth refer to this folder as the MODx root folder.

It is also important to mention the same path when referring to the CSS in the template as we have done earlier. All files are served from the MODx root folder because every page is actually rendered by `index.php`, which is stored in the MODx root folder.

Here is the relevant extract from the code given in the *HTML* section:

```
<link rel="stylesheet" type="text/css" href="assets/templates/
learningMODx/style.css" />
```

Notice the use of [*#content*] within the HTML. We will discuss it in the next section. For now, just understand that when MODx parses [*#content*], the content of the document is placed in its position in within the template, and hence it ([*#content*]) is called placeholder.

Making the Home Page use the created template

Now that you have created a new template, let us use this template for the Home Page. The steps to change the template are the same as the ones mentioned in the *Changing the template of a document* section to change the template of the document to blank. Only this time, choose the template named Learning MODx, which is the default template, instead of blank.

Click on **Preview** and the page will look similar to the following:

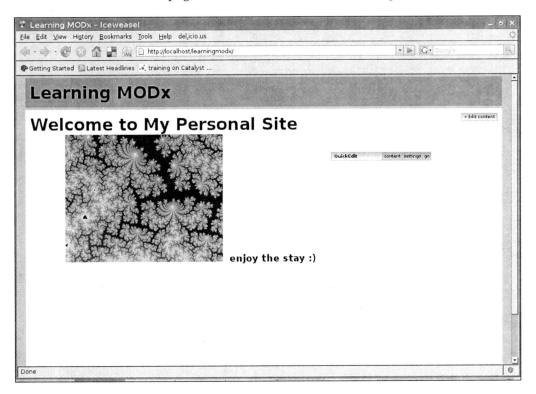

Choosing a default template

Now that we have made the Home Page use the newly created template, we might also want to use this template for most of our other pages. Let us configure MODx to use this template as the default template for all documents that will henceforth be created:

1. Open the MODx site configuration as explained in the previous chapter.

2. Change the option **Default Template** from the drop-down box to the newly created template.

3. Click **Save.**

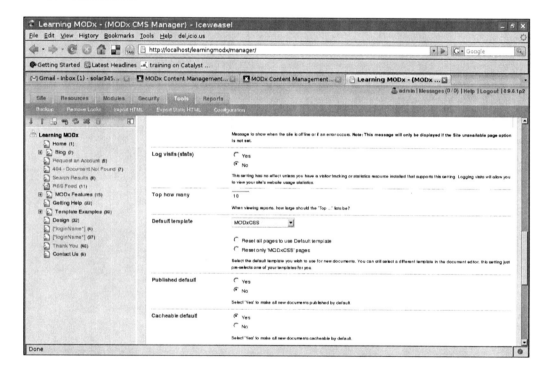

Introducing template variables

Template variables give life to otherwise static layouts. They allow templates to have dynamic content. You have already seen an example of document-specific template variable when you used [*#content*] in the template that you created in the last section. Template variables are entities that may have different values in different pages for different users at different times. They can be embedded in a template or in a document's content to display the value that they store. The value of a template variable can generally be shown in a template by enclosing the name of the template variable within [* and *], like [*template variable name*]. This is a good time to check out the code of the templates that came with the sample site when MODx was installed to consolidate your understanding of what is happening. When reading through the code, you might encounter syntax for template variables like [*#templatevariablename*]. This syntax is used when you want to be able to edit the content using the quickedit module. Template variables are created and assigned to documents as we will see in the next section.

Besides the template variables that are explicitly created, all documents have certain values that are accessible as document-specific variables. These variables contain information about the document, such as the content of the document, name, description, who it was created by, and so on.

Modifying the template to add dynamic behavior

We have now created the template that renders the content of the document at a specific location. Let us now extend it, using our newly acquired knowledge of template variables, to also show the document title. The document-specific variable for this is pagetitle. Modify the template by adding the highlighted segment, which we have created to contain the title, giving the following HTML:

```
<!DOCTYPE html PUBLIC "-//W3C//DTD XHTML 1.1//EN"
   "http://www.w3.org/TR/xhtml11/DTD/xhtml11.dtd">
<html xmlns="http://www.w3.org/1999/xhtml" xml:lang="en">
<head>
<title>Learning Modx</title>
<meta http-equiv="Content-Type" content="text/html; charset=iso-8859-
                                                             1" />
<link rel="stylesheet" type="text/css" href="style.css" />
</head>
<body>
<div id="banner">
<h1>Logo</h1>
</div>
<div id="wrapper">
 <div id="container">
  <div id="content">
    [*pagetitle*]
     <br/>
    [*#content*]
  </div>
 </div>
```

```
    <div class="clearing"></div>
</div> <!-- end of wrapper div -->
<div id="footer">It is fun and exciting to build websites with
                                  Modx</div></body>
</html>
```

Changing existing templates

Follow these steps to change the code of an existing template:

1. Click on the **Resources** menu in the top navigation panel.
2. Click on the **Edit Resources** menu item.
3. Click on the template to be edited—in this case, the Learning MODx default template.
4. Replace the existing HTML with the HTML given above.
5. Click on **Save** to store the changes.
6. Click on the **Preview** menu item in the **Site** menu to see the preview.

You will see something like this:

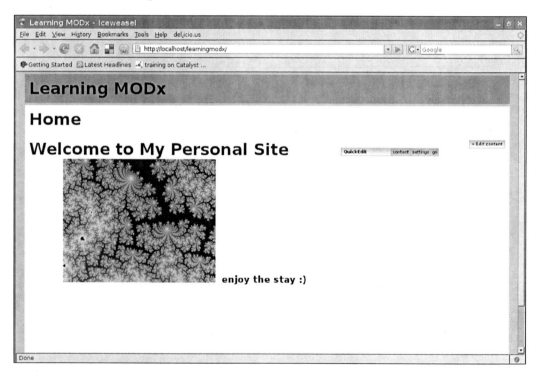

As you can see, the template now displays the page title before the content.

Template variables

We have already discussed a special type of template variables called document-specific variables.

In this section, we will cover the creation of template variables that are specific to templates. We will be using the concepts covered here throughout the book for practical examples. This section provides you with a theoretical background that eases the understanding when using template variables in the corresponding chapters. To explain template variables, let us consider a blog site. Each blog entry can have some values attached to it, such as a tag and a rating. A tag is just a value assigned to a blog page that specifies which category this blog page belongs to, and a rating allows the visitors to rate the quality of the blog. All these values, which can be different for each document, can be stored using template variables. Hence a template variable is a property of a template that has individual values for each document using the template. In this section, you will learn the following:

- How to create template variables
- The types of values that a template variable can store
- Different ways that you can allow a user to change the value of a template variable
- Different sources from which template variables can take their value
- Different presentational methods for the value of template variables

Creating template variables

In this section, you will learn how to create template variables and their various properties, in detail. Start creating your template variable by following these steps:

1. Click on the **Resources** menu in the top navigation panel.
2. Click on the **Manage Resources** menu item.
3. Click on the **Template Variables** tab in the right content area.
4. Click on **New Template Variable**.

Data source binding

Data source bindings allow the input option values and the default value to be retrieved from an external source like a file or a database. This can be helpful when there are a lot of values, or values that will change with the time. The following is a list of keywords that function as a data source when used in these fields:

- @FILE — gets the data from the contents of the specified file; for example, @FILE colors.txt.

- @DOCUMENT — gets the data from the contents of the given document ID; for example, @DOCUMENT 22.

- @CHUNK — gets the data from the contents of the given chunk. Chunks are discussed in the following sections.

- @SELECT — gets the data by querying the database.

- @EVAL — gets the data from the result returned by the given PHP code

- @INHERIT — gets the data from the given content. If no content is given, it looks for the content of the same variable in the parent document, and so on, and continues to the root document until it finds a value.

Widgets

Widgets format the output of the template variable to be displayed on the final web page. So Input Type determines what will be displayed when editing the document, and Widgets determine what will be displayed in the final web page output.

The following is a list of the available widgets in MODx:

- Data Grid
- Floater
- Marquee
- RichText
- Ticker
- View Port
- HTML Entities
- Date Formatter
- Unixtime
- Delimited List

- HTML Generic Tag
- Hyperlink
- Image
- String Formatter

Each of these options has configurations attached to it. Certain widget options will be explained in detail as we use them in the remaining chapters.

Creating a blog site

Now that we have created a template, we can create any number of documents that can use the same template. Now let us extend this behavior further to allow a user to create a document using some interface in the site without having to use the Manager interface. In the next section, you will find the required theory behind what we are going to do. All that we do here is create a document that shows a form with the fields relating to a blog post to the end user. When the end user fills in the content and submits the data, a new document is created.

Creating a document

We will now create a document to show a basic blog from and process the posted data. Create the new document by clicking on the new document icon in the left panel.

Populate the following fields and save the document:

Field Name	Field
Title	Post a Blog !
Long Title	Post a Blog !
Description	This page allows a user to post a blog entry
Template	Learning MODx default template (should have been selected by default)

You will find the newly created document and its assigned ID. You will be using this ID in the following steps. It will be referred to as PID.

1. Click on the document and click **Edit**.
2. Change the **Editor** of **Document Content** to **none**.
3. Fill the **Document Content** with the following content:
   ```
   [!NewsPublisher? &folder=`PID` &makefolder=`1`!]
   ```

- Use the back-tick character (`` ` ``) and not a single quote (`'`).
- There should not be any line breaks between `[!` and `!]`. In other words, do not press *Enter* in the middle of the statement. Sometimes when the string is longer, the browser displays it in multiple lines. That is fine, but there should not be line breaks.
- Replace PID with the ID of the current document. (The ID is highlighted in the following image.)

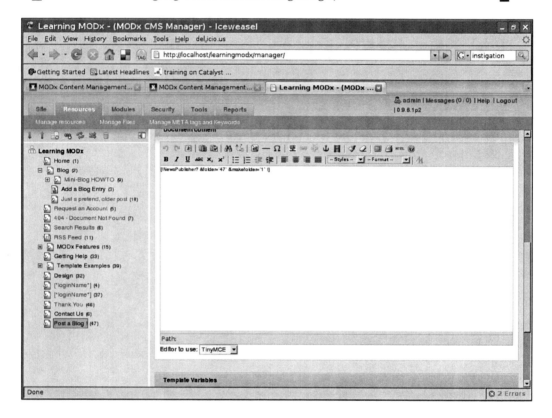

The screenshot shows the ID of the document and that being used as the PID in the snippet call.

4. Save the document.

Post a Blog ! entry

Now that you have created a mechanism to post a blog entry, let us see how it works. Right-click on the newly created document and click **Preview**. You will see a page like the following:

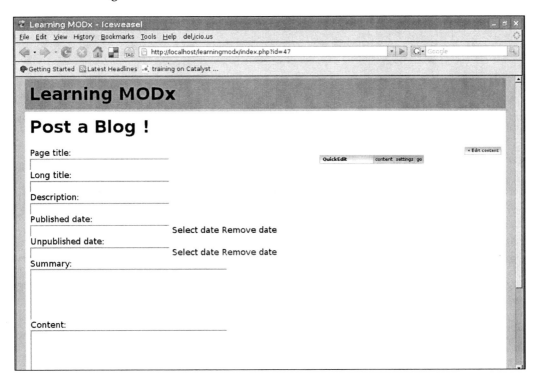

Fill in the fields with the following information and then click **Submit**.

- **Page title: My First Blog**
- **Long title: My First Blog in my own site**
- **Description: Posting a blog using the Post a Blog ! page**
- **Published date**: leave as empty
- **Unpublished date**: leave as empty
- **Summary: Blogging is fun**
- **Content: Let's all start blogging**

A new document is created and displayed.

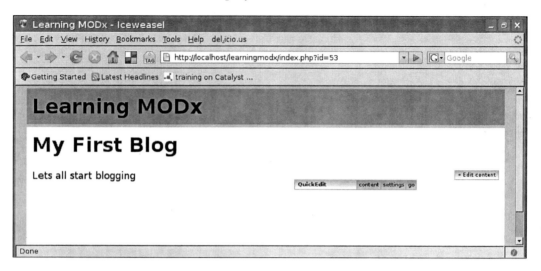

Now, in the `manager` folder, click on the refresh icon in the left panel and you will notice that the blog creation page has turned into a folder with a + symbol. If you click on it, you will see that it contains the newly created document.

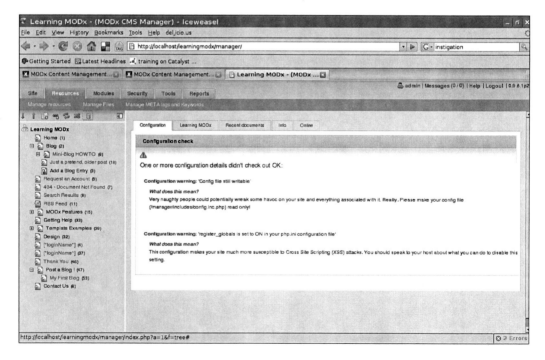

You have successfully created a basic blog interface and have also posted a blog entry. It is time to understand what is happening and to tweak the interface a bit.

Snippet and chunk basics

Snippets are executable PHP code that provides some functionality when called.

In the previous example, `NewsPublisher` is a snippet. The only content of the **Post a Blog !** page was the call to the `NewsPublisher` snippet; the snippet takes care of displaying a form and storing the values entered through it as a new document. There is a whole chapter on *Snippets* in this book (Chapter 8). In this section, you will learn the bare minimum about snippets that is necessary to follow along in the consecutive chapters.

Generating output

Most snippets return an output that gets shown in the template at the same location where the call to the snippet was made.

Such output can be returned by snippets in two ways:

- **Return the HTML**: In this method, there is less control over what the snippet returns. Changes in the returned output can only be made by editing the snippet code, as the snippet has the HTML that has to be returned within the snippet code.
- **Use chunks**: Snippets can render an output using chunks that use place holders in the same way that a template does. The snippet can create these placeholders and store values in them. When a snippet uses chunks to render output, each placeholder that the chunk will be using is created and its value is assigned by the template. Then the template renders a chunk by replacing the placeholders in the chunk with their values.

Let us look into the call we made to the `NewsPublisher` again.

```
[!NewsPublisher? &folder=`PID` &makefolder=`1`!]
```

There are a few things to note here:

- Calls to snippets can be made by enclosing the snippet name within `[!` and `!]`
- A snippet can accept parameters that can alter its behavior, such as `folder` and `makefolder` in the last example
- Such parameters are passed as a key and value pair in the format `key=value`

- The snippet name and the parameters are separated by the ? symbol, which follows immediately after the snippet name

- Every parameter has an & symbol appended to the key

- The values of all parameters are within the ` symbol

Snippet calls can also be made by enclosing the snippet name within [[ ]]. The difference between [[ ]] and [! !] is that the former is cached and the latter is uncached. Caching is a technique to improve performance by saving a processed value to avoid processing on further calls. In MODx, the documents can be cached. When we use the uncached notation for calling snippets, the snippet will still be processed to ensure that the content of the snippet is always dynamic even in a cached page. In an uncached page, the snippet is always processed irrespective of the notation.

NewsPublisher is a snippet that displays a form and stores the posted information as a document. It can be configured to work in many different ways depending on the parameters passed along. We will discuss this in more detail in the chapter on *Snippets*. The few parameters that are of interest in this chapter are explained below.

- folder—specifies under which container the newly created documents should be placed

- makefolder—if the given value for the parameter above is only a document and not a container, the value in this parameter controls whether the document is converted to a container automatically

- formtpl—a customized form is shown from a chunk specified with this parameter

- rtcontent—when this is specified, the given field will be treated as rich text instead of raw text

- Template—the document that is created by NewsPublisher will use the template mentioned here

Having created a simple blog interface, we are going to do two enhancements using what we have learned, which will be explained in the following sections.

Using a custom form for the Post a Blog ! page

To customize the form, all we need to do is create a form in HTML, save it as a chunk, and pass the name of this chunk as the value of `formtpl` to `NewsPublisher`.

We need a mechanism by which we can let the `NewsPublisher` snippet know which text field, from the document, gets stored as which property. For example, we might have a title, summary, and content, and we will want the title to be saved as the document-specific variable `longtitle`, the summary as the document-specific variable description, and the content field as the content of the document. This has to be explicitly specified, as `NewsPublisher` has no method to make guesses about which field gets stored as what in the document.

When using a chunk as a form template along with `NewsPublisher`, the specification of what field gets stored as what variable in the document is done by setting the name attribute of the form element to the document-specific variable. The following is the HTML for the custom blog form. There are more concepts to discuss on snippets like NewsPublisher and how to use chunks with them. They are dealt with in the later chapters.

HTML for the custom blog form

The following is the code for the chunk that will be used by the `NewsPublisher` snippet to render a custom form.

```
<div id="blogpage">
<form action="[~[*id*]~]" method="post" name="NewsPublisher">
 <table>
  <h3> Blog Entry </h3>
  <br />
  <input name="NewsPublisherForm" type="hidden" value="on" />
 </table>
 <table>
  <tbody>
   <tr>
    <td><label for="pagetitle">Title</label></td>
    <td> <input id="pagetitle" name="pagetitle" size="40"
              type="text" value="[+pagetitle+]" /></td>
   </tr>
   <tr>
    <td><label for="introtext">Summary </label></td>
    <td><textarea cols="50" name="introtext"
```

```
       rows="5">[+introtext+]</textarea></td>
  </tr>
  <tr>
   <td><label for="content">Content</label></td>
   <td> <textarea cols="50" name="content"
       rows="5">[+content+]</textarea></td>
  </tr>
 </tbody>
 </table>
 <input class="button" name="send" type="submit" value="Blog it!" />
 </form>
 </div>
```

Steps to create a chunk

Now that we have the HTML ready for the chunk, we will create the chunk in this section.

1. Click on the **Manage Resources** menu item in the **Resources** menu.

2. Click on the **Chunks** tab, and click on **New Chunk.**

3. Fill in the following data in the new chunk page.

Field Name	Value
Chunk name	blogform
Description	Form template for posting a blog
Existing Category	Learning MODx
Chunk code	The HTML above
Editor to use	None

4. Click on the **Save** button.

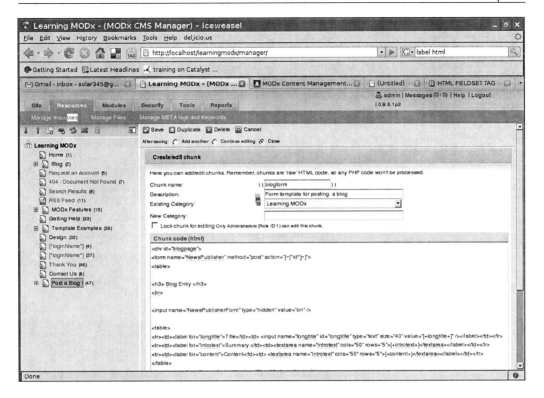

Using a chunk as a form template

The following are the steps to make `NewsPublisher` use the created chunk as the form template:

1. Click on the **Post a Blog !** document and click **Edit.**

2. Replace the document content with the following:

   ```
   [!NewsPublisher? &folder=`47` &makefolder=`1` &formtpl=`blogform`
                    &template=`Learning MODx blog template`!]
   ```

3. Click on the **Save** button.

Also, as you can guess from the snippet call, we are creating a new template for all blogs. For now, this template will be the same as the `Learning MODx` default template. To create the template:

1. Open the `Learning MODx blog` template from **Templates** in the **Manage Resources** submenu.

2. Click on **Duplicate**, and click **Yes** when asked.

3. Change the template name to `Learning MODx blog` template.

4. Select the **Category** as **Learning MODx.**

5. Click **Save.**

Checking the Post a Blog ! page

Now that we are using a custom form template, let us check if it works.

1. Right-click on the **Post a Blog !** page and click on **Preview.**

2. Fill in the fields with the following content and click on the **Blog it!** button.

Field Name	Value
Title	My Second Blog Entry
Summary	Just created a custom blog template
Content	It is simple and quick to allow well written snippets to take advantage of custom formatting using chunks

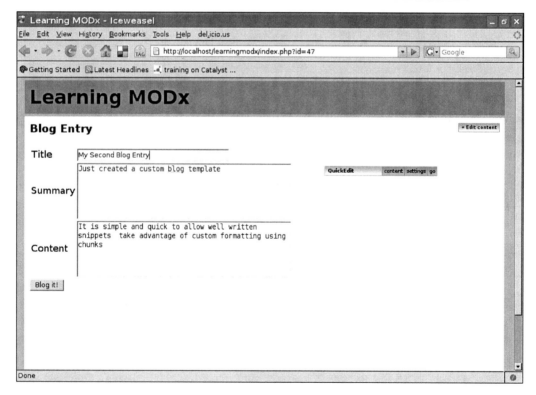

You will see the posted blog entry in a new page:

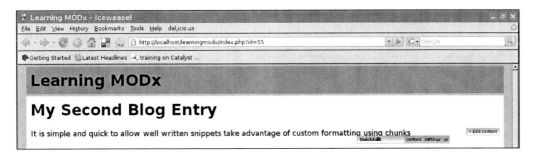

Rich text editor for the blog content

To provide a rich text editor for the blog content area, all that has to be done is to replace the content area with a template variable that is of the rich text type and uses the rich text widget. This way, MODx gives a rich text editor when the form is being filled in or edited. This is a three step process:

- Creation of the template variable
- Making the form template chunk use the template variable
- Letting NewsPublisher be aware that the news content field has changed to the new template variable

Creating the template variable

1. Click on the **Manage Resources** menu item in the **Resources** menu.
2. Click on the **Template Variables** tab, and click on **New Template Variable.**
3. Fill in the fields with the following values:

Field Name	Value
Variable Name	BlogRT
Description	Template Variable to store rich text for the blogs
Input Type	Rich Text
Widget	Rich Text
Widget width	100%
Widget height	300px
Editor	TinyMCE
Template Access	Learning MODx default template
Existing Category	Learning MODx

4. Click on **Save.**

Chunk and template variable

Now that we have created a template variable with the rich text widget, let us modify the form template to use it.

The HTML of the `blogform` chunk has to be replaced with the following.

```
<div id="blogpage">
<form action="[~[*id*]~]" method="post" name="NewsPublisher">
 <table>
  <h3> Blog Entry </h3>
  <br />
  <input name="NewsPublisherForm" type="hidden" value="on" />
 </table>
 <table>
  <tbody>
   <tr>
    <td><label for="pagetitle">Title</label></td>
    <td> <input id="pagetitle" name="pagetitle" size="40" type="text"
                                    value="[+pagetitle+]" /></td>
   </tr>
   <tr>
    <td><label for="introtext">Summary </label></td>
    <td><textarea cols="50" name="introtext"
      rows="5">[+introtext+]</textarea></td>
   </tr>
   <tr>
    <td><label for="content">Content</label></td>
    <td> [*blogRT*]</td>
   </tr>
  </tbody>
 </table>
 <input class="button" name="send" type="submit" value="Blog it!" />
</form>
</div>
```

Instead of calling a form field, such as `textarea`, with the name of the document-specific variable, we have replaced that line with a call to the template variable (see highlighted line in the previous code). This single line performs all the necessary functionalities to make the template variable editable, using the selected widget according to the content type.

To replace the previous HTML in the form template chunk, do the following:

1. Click on the **Manage Resources** menu item in the **Resources** menu.
2. Click on the **Chunks** tab.
3. Click on the **blogform** chunk.
4. Replace the HTML in the Chunk Code area with the previous HTML.
5. Click on **Save**.

Now, right-click on the **Post a Blog !** page, click **Preview**, and you will see something like this:

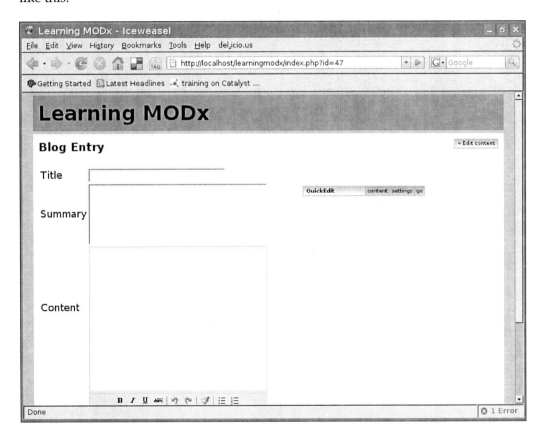

NewsPublisher and the Rtcontent field

You have now enabled the content field to use the rich text editor. But `NewsPublisher` is still expecting the blog content to come from a form field with the name **Content**. Hence, when it is saving the form, it will throw a validation error stating that the news content is missing. When you try to post a blog entry now, the following is the error that you will get:

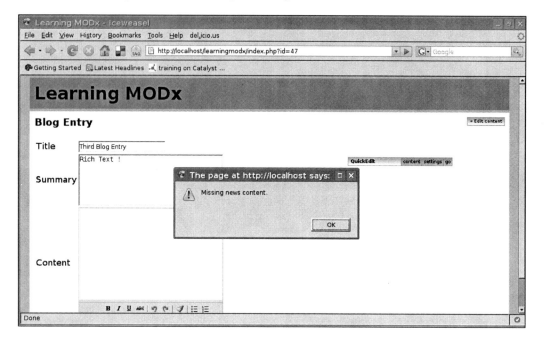

We can set this right by passing the value of the new template variable using the `rtcontent` parameter.

To do that, edit the **Post a Blog !** page as mentioned in the previous sections and replace the code with the following:

```
[!NewsPublisher? &folder=`47` &makefolder=`1` &formtpl=`blogform`
                                        &rtcontent=`tvblogRT` !]
```

Save the document and preview it.

Now you will be able to use the rich text editor for the content area and post blogs. Go ahead and post a few blogs to check if it works.

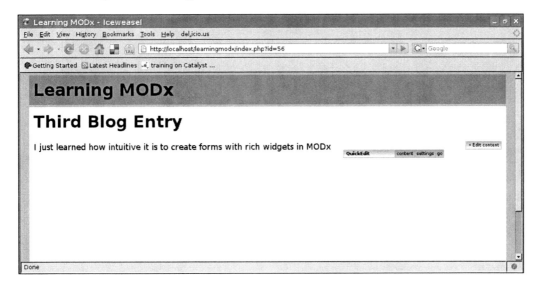

Summary

In this chapter, you have learned about:

- Templates
  - Creation/addition
  - Flow of rendering

- Template variables and Document Specific variables
  - Data Types
  - Widgets
  - Data Sources

- Snippets and chunks briefly

You have also, during the process, created:

- A template for the site
- Blog functionality
- custom form template for the blog page
- rich text editor for the blog

5
Authentication and Authorization

Authentication is the process of verifying that users are who they claim to be. Authorization is the process of granting access to the authenticated users—based on their role—to perform operations such as view, edit, or delete on resources. In this chapter, you will learn how MODx facilitates authentication and authorization. You will build your site to include user registrations, logins, user types, and set rules on who can do what.

As you read this chapter, it is important that you keep in mind that MODx has two user types.

- Web Users—users who use the web site
- Manager Users—users who are allowed to log in to the Manager interface

It is vital to keep this distinction in mind to be able to understand the complexities explained in this chapter.

You will also learn in this chapter how MODx allows grouping of documents, users, and permissions.

Create web users

Let us start by creating a web user. Web users are users who can access restricted document groups in the web site frontend; they do not have Manager access.

Web users can identify themselves at login by using login forms. They are allowed to log in from the user page, but they cannot log in using the Manager interface. To create a web user, perform the following steps:

1. Click on the **Web Users** menu item in the **Security** menu.

2. Click on **New Web User**.

3. Fill in the fields with the following information:

Field Name	Value
Username	samira
Password	samira123
Email Address	xyz@configurelater.com

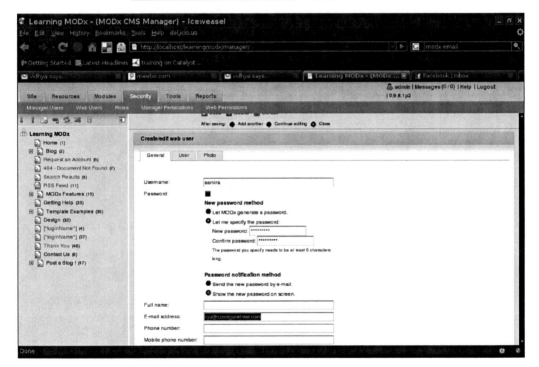

4. Click on the **Save** button.

Now you will see a page like the following, which lists all the web users on your site.

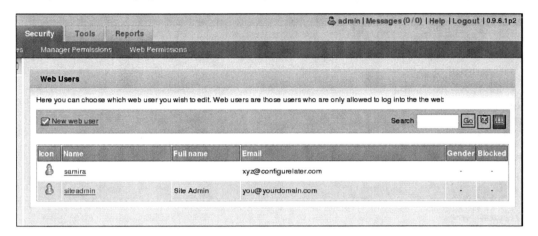

Other user properties

There are other fields that you can fill in, such as the name, address, and so on, in the **General** tab. There is also a **Photo** tab, where you can upload a picture for a user.

In the **User** tab, you have the following fields:

- **Login Home Page**: Here you can specify the document that the user is shown immediately after login.

- **Allowed IP Address**: It is possible to allow certain users to log in only from specific machines. This can be set for the particular user by specifying the IP numbers of the machines in this field separated by a comma.

- **Allowed Days**: It is possible to allow certain users to log in only on certain days of the week. This can be set for the particular user by selecting which days the user is allowed to log in.

When you click on any user on the web users' page, a page opens that allows you to edit the existing information and also shows simple statistics, such as when the user last logged in. It is also possible to block or unblock the particular user from this page. You can also set **Blocked Until** or **Blocked After** to block a user for a certain period and to schedule such a block. When a user is blocked, MODx does not allow that user to log in.

Add the login snippet

Now that we have created a user, let us add a login form that allows the user to log in to the site.

This process is very simple. All that you have to do is call the WebLogin snippet in the template where you want the login page to be shown. We are going to change the template HTML with the following HTML for the Learning MODx default template:

```
<!DOCTYPE html PUBLIC "-//W3C//DTD XHTML 1.1//EN" "http://www.w3.org/
TR/xhtml11/DTD/xhtml11.dtd"> <html xmlns="http://www.w3.org/1999/
xhtml" xml:lang="en">
 <head>
  <base href="[(site_url)]"></base>
  <title>Learning MODx</title>
  <meta http-equiv="Content-Type" content="text/html; charset=iso-
                                        8859-1" />
```

```
      <link rel="stylesheet" type="text/css" href="style.css" />
   </head>
   <body>
    <div id="banner">
     <h1>Learning MODx</h1>
    </div>
    <div id="wrapper">
     <div id="container">
      <div id="content">
        <div id="col-1">
         <h1>[*pagetitle*]</h1>
         <br/>
         [*#content*]
        </div>
        <div id="col-2" >
         <div > [!WebLogin!] </div>
        </div>
      </div>
     </div>
     <div class="clearing"> </div>
    </div> <!-- end of wrapper div -->
    <div id="footer">It is fun and exciting to build websites with
                                        MODx</div></body>
   </html>
```

Notice that the only addition is the call to the [!WebLogin!] snippet besides the change in the HTML layout, which now has two divs id=col-1 and id=col-2 within the div with id=content to make the content area into two panes.

Also, since we have made changes to the layout, we will have to change the style.css file to specify the width of col-1 and col-2. The new style.css should be changed to:

```
* { padding:2; margin:0; border:1; }
body { margin:0 20px; background:#8CEC81; }
#banner { background: #2BB81B; border-top:5px solid #8CEC81; border-
                                       bottom:5px solid #8CEC81; }
#banner h1 { padding:10px; }
#wrapper { background: #8CEC81; }
#container { width: 100%; background: #2BB81B; float: left; }
#content { background: #ffffff; height:600px; padding:0 10px 10px
                                       10px; clear:both; }
#footer { background: #2BB81B; border-top:5px solid #8CEC81; border-
                                       bottom:5px solid #8CEC81; }
.clearing { clear:both; height:0; }
```

```
#content #col-1 {float:left;width:500px; margin:0px;padding:0px;}
#content #col-2 {float:right; width:300px; margin:0px; padding:30px 0
          10px 25px; border-left:3px solid #99cc66; height:500px;}
#content #col-2 div {padding-bottom:20px;}
```

The following are the steps to change the template to use a login snippet and to style it as described above:

1. Click on the **Manage Resources** menu item of the **Resources** menu.

2. Click on the **Learning MODx** default template.

3. Replace it with the preceding HTML.

4. Click on **Save**.

5. Open the style.css file that you created earlier from the learningMODx folder.

6 Replace it with the preceding and save the file.

Now preview the Home Page; it should look similar to this:

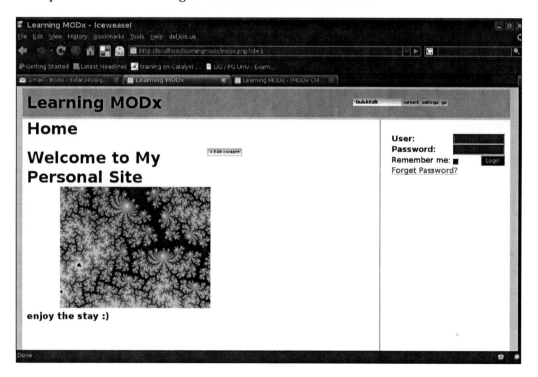

Log in as **samira**. The screen will now look something like the following:

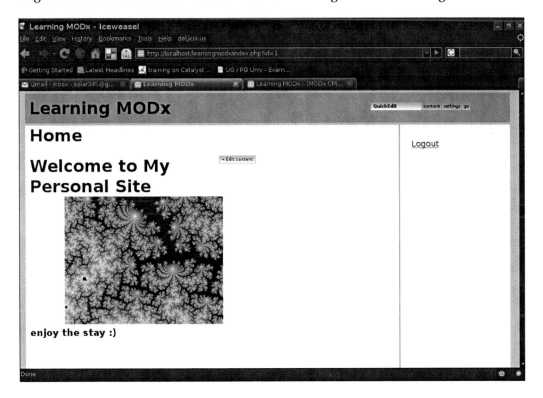

Notice that the **QuickEdit** bar is dependent on whom you log in as from the Manager interface and not on whom you log in as from the Web interface. You can check this out by clicking on the **Logout** link in the Manager page and refreshing the Home Page. The QuickEdit bar does not appear.

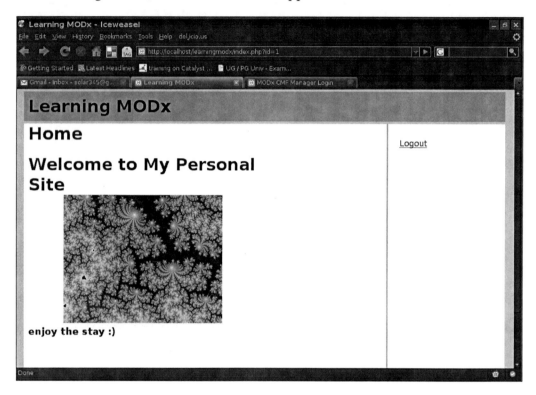

Documents can be assigned to document groups and permissions can be defined on document groups. In our site, we want only our friends to post a blog, though anyone can write a comment. So we will create a user group called Friends and assign all the friends that we will allow to blog to this group.

Perform the following steps to create the Friends user group:

1.   Click on the **Web Permissions** menu item on the **Security** menu.
2.   Click on the **Web User groups** tab if it is not the default selected tab.
3.   In the **Create a new user group** box, type **Friends**.
4.   Click on **Submit**.

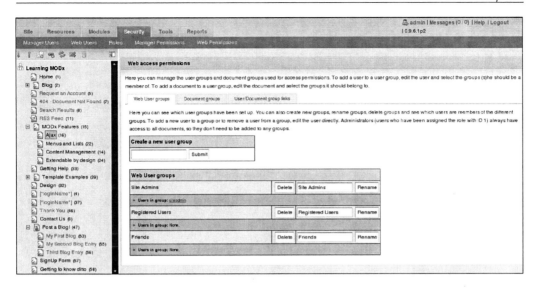

Document group for friends

Now that we have a user group called Friends, we need to specify which, otherwise not accessible, documents are accessible by this group. We can group all those documents into a document group. The following are the steps to create a document group:

1. Click on the **Web Permissions** menu item on the **Security** menu.
2. Click on the **Document groups** tab if it is not the default selected tab.
3. In the **Create a new document group** box, type **onlyforfriends**.
4. Click on **Submit**.

Restricting access for a document

All the documents so far have been created as **All Document Groups (Public)**.This means that anybody can access the documents. When we assign a document to some other group, then only the users belonging to that particular group can access it. Now let us change the document group of **Post a Blog** to **onlyforfriends** as follows:

1. Click on the **Post a Blog!** document from the document tree.

2. Click on the **Edit** button.

3. Click on the **Page Settings** tab.

4. Click on the **onlyforfriends** checkbox under the **Access Permissions** heading at the bottom of the page.

5. Click on the **Save** button.

User group: Document group

If you have logged in as samira from the web site, log off and preview the Post a Blog! page. You will still see the blog page. This is because when we assign a document to a document group, it is still accessible to everyone. Only when a user group is linked to a document group do the permissions become exclusive to that group. Now let us link the Friends user group to the **onlyforfriends** document group.

1. Click on the **Web Permissions** menu item of the **Security** menu.

2. Click on the **User/Document group links**.

3. Select the **onlyforfriends** group from the drop-down box next to the **Friends** user group and click **Add**.

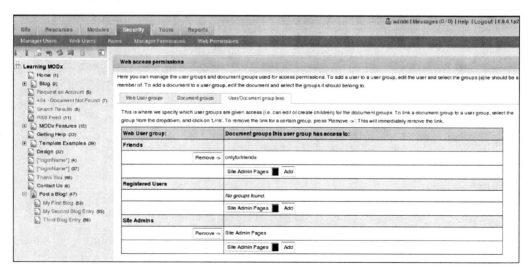

User: User group

Now preview the Post a Blog! page again and you will see something like this:

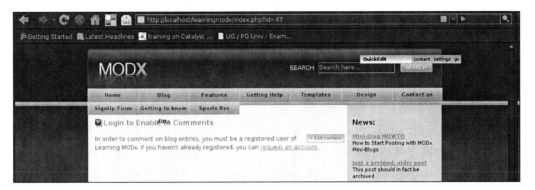

Forget about the inappropriate message for now; we will deal with it at the end of the chapter. What you must understand now is that MODx has denied access to this page, and has redirected the user to the permission denied page that was initially set in the site configuration.

Try logging in as samira from the Home Page and visiting the Post a Blog! page again. You are still unauthorized to view the page. samira can only access the Post a Blog! page if samira is a member of the Friends user group. This is because we mapped the Friends user group to the onlyforfriends document group and Post a Blog! belongs to the onlyforfriends document group. So let us go ahead and add samira to the Friends user group.

1. Click on the **Web Users** menu item of the **Security** menu.
2. Click on the username **samira**.
3. Click on the **General** tab if it was not selected already.
4. Select the **Friends** checkbox in the **Web access permissions** section.
5. Click on **Save**.

Now having logged in as samira from the Home Page, visit the Post a Blog! page. You should be able to see the regular blog page.

Post moderation

It will be helpful if we can delegate the role of moderating blogs to someone else. The user must only be able to manipulate the documents from the Manager interface and not perform any other activity. There are two points to note here:

- Able to manipulate documents from the Manager interface — must be a Manager user type
- Not able to perform any other activity — create a custom role only for manipulating documents

Creating a role

Let us create a role called Blog Moderators who can only edit documents.

1. Click on the **Roles** menu item of the **Security** menu.
2. Click on **Create/edit role** and fill in the following information:

Field Name	Field Value
Role name	Blog Moderators
Description	Role type that allows only administration of documents

3. Have the following checkboxes clicked in **Content management**:
- **Edit a document**
- **Delete documents**

4. Click on the **Save** button.

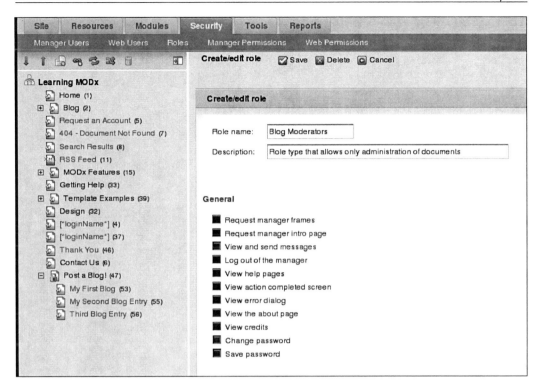

Creating a Manager user

Let us create a Manager user called blogmoderator1 who will moderate all the blogs:

1. Click on the **Manager Users** menu item in the **Security** menu.
2. Click on **New User** and fill in the following information:

Field Name	Field Value
Username	blogmoderator1
Password	blogmoderator1
Email	asd@configurelater.com
Role	Blog Moderators

3. Click on the **Save** button

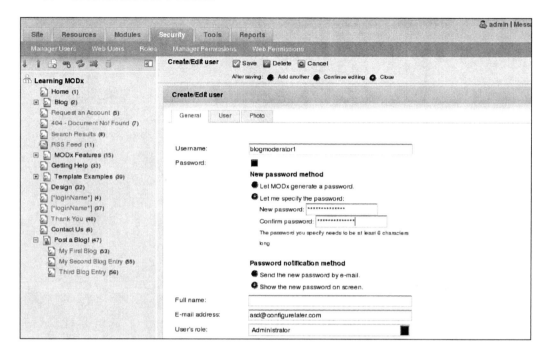

Checking the new role

Now that you have created a new role, and have assigned a user to that role, let us try to log in as that user. First, log out from the Manager interface and log in again with the username **blogmoderator1** and password **blogmoderator1**. You will see a screen like the following:

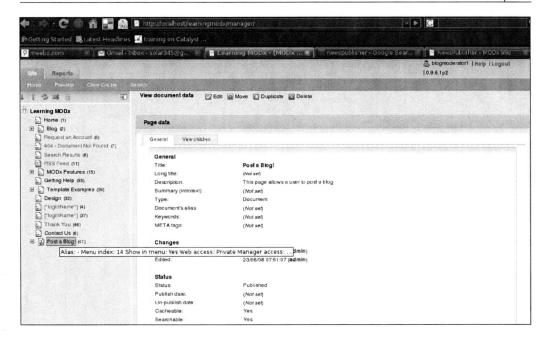

As you can see, you have been able to log in to the Manager interface successfully. And you will also notice that you are allowed to do only the activities that were enabled for this user.

User registration

We have already seen how new users can be created. Besides creating users from the Manager interface, users can also be allowed to register from a Web interface. Users who registered from the Web interface can also be assigned to a default user group.

Showing a signup form

To show a signup form, we will use a snippet that comes bundled with MODx.

1. Create a new document and fill in the following information:

Field Name	Value
Title	Signup Form
Uses Template	Learning MODx default template
Document Content	[!websignup!]

2. Click on the **Save** button.

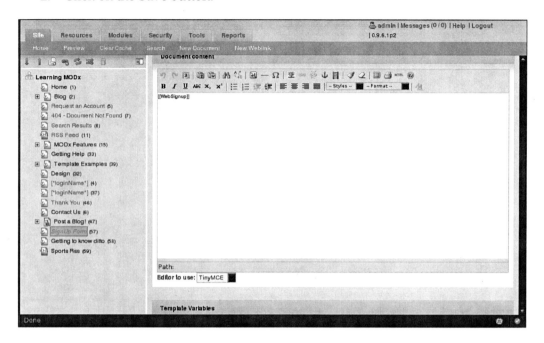

Notice that the content of the document is only `[!websignup!]`, which is a call to the snippet `websignup` that displays a user registration form.

Now preview the page and it will look like the following:

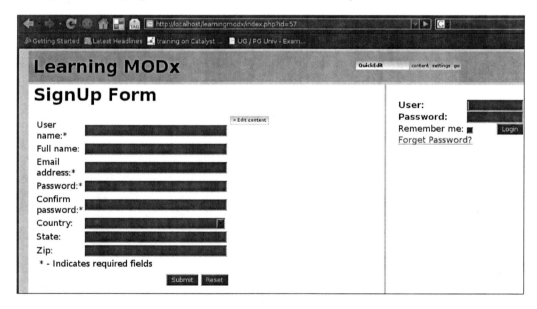

Joining a default group

To assign the registering users to the Friends user group, change the Document Content field on the sign up form to the following:

```
[!WebSignup? &groups=`Registered Users`!]
```

Notice that this functionality allows `websignup` to be called multiple times, with different parameters to have separate login forms for different kinds of users. You can even have different forms by setting a template parameter for the rendered forms.

Link the signup form in the log in snippet

Now that we have created a User Registration page, we need to add a link to the signup page. Add the following code at the end of the document Home Page:

```
<br/><a href="[~57~]">Register</a>
```

We are just creating a link to the signup page in our Home Page.

Now the Home Page will appear like the following:

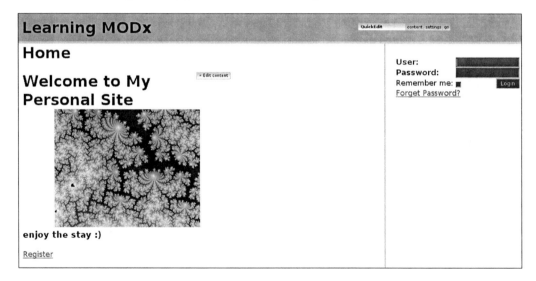

Snippets and authorization

So far, we have seen authentication and authorization with respect to:

- Web users and documents
- Managers and roles

Authorization on a document level restricts access or grants permission to a user for the entire document. Authorization within snippets can make this more granular by restricting only certain content within a document that is being rendered by the snippet. As explained in the previous chapter, snippets accept parameters, and certain snippets provide parameters to be configured so that they are accessible only by a certain user type. In this section, we will modify the NewsPublisher snippet to allow posts from only the authenticated users.

NewsPublisher and authentication

Edit the contents of the Post a Blog! page and change the document's content to the following:

```
[!NewsPublisher? &folder=`47` &makefolder=`1` &canpost=`Friends`!]
```

Now, only the registered users will be able to submit the posts. You can check this out by logging out and visiting a blog page. It will look like the following:

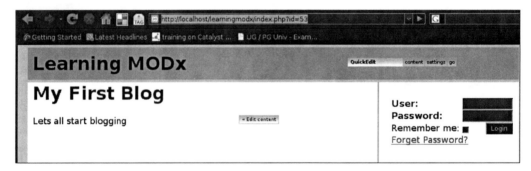

Summary

There are two categories of MODx users:

- Manager
- Web

We learned that:

- Users are grouped into User groups
- Documents can be assigned to Document groups
- Linking Document groups to Web User groups will control viewing of the documents
- Linking Document groups to Manager User groups will control Manager Access to the documents
- Roles define what the manager can do with the accessible documents

We have modified the site to have a signup form and a login form. We have also enabled blogs to be posted only by friends.

6
Content Aggregation

We have created documents, grouped them in folders, and shown them within templates. Now let us look further into showing short extracts from contents on various criteria such as the most recent or the most viewed, documents. This is generally known as content aggregation. Content aggregation extends beyond just displaying extracts from the documents in a web page and makes it possible to display the updates on the content in the site to other applications or to other web sites. In this chapter, as we build the site, we will look in detail at the following:

- Aggregation concepts
- MODx's features for aggregation

Ditto

Content aggregation is implemented in MODx using the snippet **Ditto**. Ditto is so very useful and flexible that MODx has a separate site with documentation for this particular core snippet maintained by Mark Kaplan, the author of Ditto. This chapter discusses in detail the various parameters of this snippet. Ditto is just another snippet, so you can call it from any template or document in the same way that you call any other snippet. And like any other snippet, its functionality is flexible and configurable by passing appropriate values to the parameters. There is also the flexibility to customize the returned results using place holders.

Let's start playing with Ditto by creating a document with the title **Getting to know ditto** with the content of the document as:

```
[!Ditto!]
```

Save this document and preview the page. Now, if you click **Preview**, you will see something like the following:

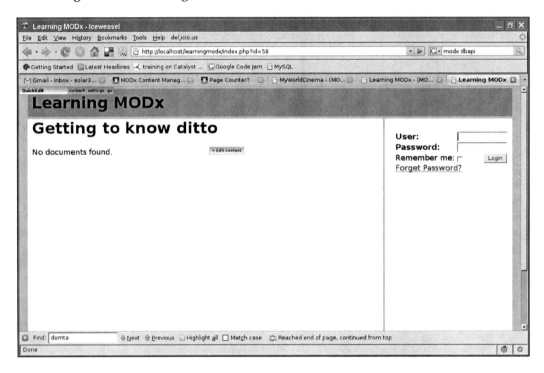

More flexibility with parameters

The screenshot suggests that Ditto has not found any documents. Of course it has not, as we have not specified where to look for the documents. When we do not specify where to look for the documents, Ditto searches by default within the current document. The current document is not a container that has other documents. There are two parameters to tell Ditto which documents' contents must be aggregated:

- Parents: List of parent documents; the children of the parents will be aggregated
- Documents: List of individual documents to be aggregated

You can specify a list of documents that must be aggregated using the `documents` parameter, or you can specify a list of container documents using the `parents` parameter. When you specify a list of container documents, all of the child documents of the containers will be aggregated.

Let us now modify the document created in the previous section to use the Post a Blog! container as the parent from which all the documents must be aggregated.

```
[!Ditto? &parents=`47`!]
```

Replace 47 with whatever the document ID of your Post a Blog! document is. Now click on **Preview** and you will see something like this:

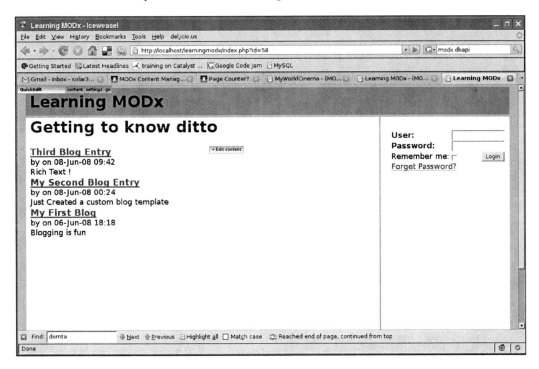

As you can see, all the documents from the container Post a Blog! are displayed with the most recently posted document first. Of course, the sorting order can be changed by passing the appropriate values to the corresponding parameters.

Aggregated data in a template

Now that we have created a document that aggregates data, let us make the last five blogs appear in every page. We can do this by introducing the Ditto call within the Learning MODx default template. The call to Ditto would look like this:

```
[!Ditto? &parents=`47`!]
```

To make the changes, replace the contents of the Learning MODx default template with the following:

```
<!DOCTYPE html PUBLIC "-//W3C//DTD XHTML 1.1//EN" "http://www.w3.org/
TR/xhtml11/DTD/xhtml11.dtd"> <html xmlns="http://www.w3.org/1999/
xhtml" xml:lang="en">
 <head>
  <title>Learning MODx</title>
  <meta http-equiv="Content-Type" content="text/html; charset=iso-
                                            8859-1" />
  <link rel="stylesheet" type="text/css" href="style.css" />
 </head>
 <body>
  <div id="banner">
   <h1>Learning MODx</h1>
  </div>
[!Wayfinder!]
  <div id="wrapper">
   <div id="container">
    <div id="content">
     <div id="col-1">
      <h1>[*pagetitle*]</h1>
      <br/>
      [*#content*]
     </div>
     <div id="col-2" >
      <div > [!WebLogin!] </div>
       <div>
         [!Ditto? &parents=`47`!]
       </div>
      </div>
     </div>
    </div>
   </div>
   <div class="clearing"> </div>
  </div> <!-- end of wrapper div -->
  <div id="footer">It is fun and exciting to build websites with
                                        MODx</div></body>
 </html>
```

Click on **Preview** and you will see something like the following:

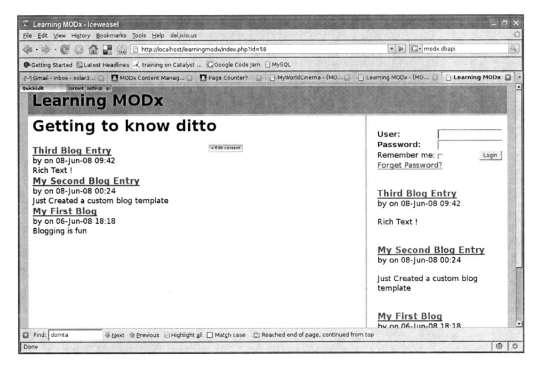

Theming MODx—chunks and placeholders

Ditto, like any other snippet, allows theming using placeholders. That is, instead of the snippet returning the complete HTML for each extract of a document, the snippet returns variables such as content, title, date created, author, and so on, which can be used in a custom chunk. Hence, the chunk will be called for every document that Ditto is aggregating. Whatever HTML the chunk gets processed into will be the output for that document.

Let us consider a chunk code like the following:

```
<h3><a href="[~[+id+]~]">[+title+]</a></h3>
[+introtext+]
```

The above chunk shows the title of the document with a link and the summary.

Suppose there are three documents that are aggregated by a particular Ditto call. If that call to Ditto has a parameter that mentions that the above chunk should be used as the template, then the above chunk will be processed three times, once for each document. The appropriate title and author name would be inserted.

The following is a list of some of the most commonly used Ditto placeholders.

- [+title+] — shows the title of the document
- [+summary+] — shows the summary, if it is not empty, or shows an extract from the document content
- [+link+] — creates a **Read More...** link to the document
- [+author+] — shows the name of the author in the **Created by** field
- [+id+] — shows the ID of the document

Now, let us go ahead and theme the aggregation that we have created:

1. Create a chunk with the following data:

Field Name	Value
Title	dittofrontpage
Chunk Code	From the preceding code

2. Change the Learning MODx default template to the following:

```
<!DOCTYPE html PUBLIC "-//W3C//DTD XHTML 1.1//EN" "http://www.
w3.org/TR/xhtml11/DTD/xhtml11.dtd"> <html xmlns="http://www.
w3.org/1999/xhtml" xml:lang="en">
 <head>
  <title>Learning MODx</title>
  <meta http-equiv="Content-Type" content="text/html; charset=iso-
                                    8859-1"
/>
  <link rel="stylesheet" type="text/css" href="style.css" />
 </head>
 <body>
  <div id="banner">
   <h1>Learning MODx</h1>
  </div>
[!Wayfinder!]
  <div id="wrapper">
   <div id="container">
    <div id="content">
     <div id="col-1">
      <h1>[*pagetitle*]</h1>
      <br/>
      [*#content*]
     </div>
```

```
    <div id="col-2" >
     <div > [!WebLogin!] </div>
      <div>
        [!Ditto? &parents=`47` &tpl=`dittofrontpage`!]
      </div>
     </div>
    </div>
   </div>
   <div class="clearing"> </div>
  </div> <!-- end of wrapper div -->
  <div id="footer">It is fun and exciting to build websites with
                                          MODx</div></body>
 </html>
```

Introducing tagging

Let us use what we have learned so far to allow tagging of documents in separate categories. For this, we will be:

1. Creating a template variable to hold the category of a document
2. Assigning the documents to a category
3. Creating separate documents with a Ditto call to show the most recent documents of each category

Creating a template variable to hold the category

If we want documents to be tagged, the documents must have a field that can hold the category to which they belong. Let's create a template variable that allows you to choose from a list of categories with the following details:

Field Name	Value
Variable Name	Blogcategories
Caption	Category
Input Type	Listbox(Multiple-Select)
Input Option Values	Sports || LifeStyle || IT
Template Access	Learning MODx default template
Access permissions	onlyforfriends
Category	Learning MODx

Assigning documents to a category

Now that you have created a category, let's go and change the categories of a few documents:

1. Select the document and click **Edit**
2. Select the category from the drop-down box in the template variable section
3. Click on **Save**

Repeat the above steps for all the blogs that you have created. Now that we have created tags, we can explore how to use them. But before that, we will have a quick look at the XML formats.

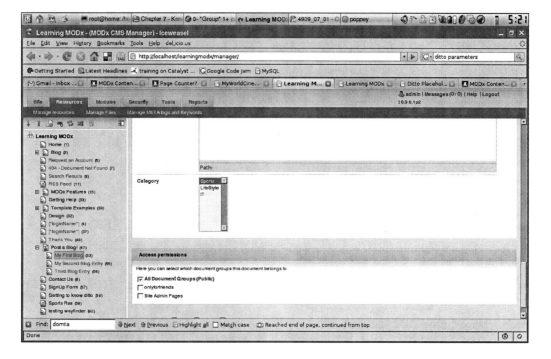

XML formats

It is really interesting that we have three documents that aggregate and display the blogs belonging to one of the three categories that we have defined. This alone can be useful to show the recent posts of a site from each category. But this can be extended further to be more useful, by allowing these documents to render the documents in a way that machines understand. We want the documents to be able to be processed and displayed by other web sites, or to be able to be read by the news feed readers.

Machine-readable formats and readers

XML is about defining document definition tags on the fly and placing the data within such tags. Unlike HTML, there is no fixed set of such tags. Hence, to make sense of such tags, the machine reading them must have some prior knowledge of what those tags mean. Groups of such definitions in a specific order and convention are called **Formats**. We have many such formats that are commonly used for sharing data. We also have what are called **Readers**. Readers are web sites or applications that process the content in a known format and present it to the user in a usable format. A common example of such a reader is the Google news reader or Gnus mode in Emacs.

Readers

A typical reader asks for a **Feed**. A feed is a URL from which the reader can fetch the data. A reader would consist of different links or buttons for each feed, which, when clicked on, show the titles of the documents. The users can read the document they wish to, by clicking on its title.

The following screenshots show **Google Reader** as an example of an RSS reader and feed list:

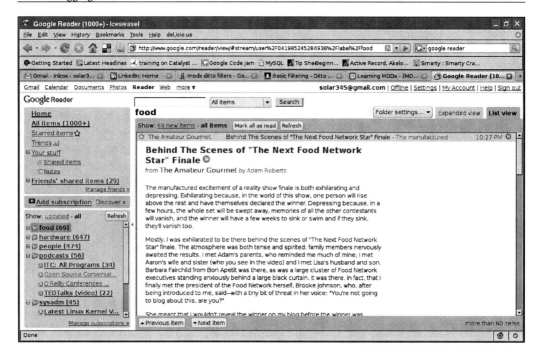

Formats

As discussed above, there are various XML formats that most readers understand. Below is a brief description of them.

- **RSS**: **Really Simple Syndication** is the most commonly used format for reading news. Each document represents an article. An article has a title, description, link, and contents.

- **Atom**: Same as RSS, but fixes many limitations of RSS. Also, this format can keep track of article updates by registering the timestamps of modification.

- **JSON**: This format is widely used for cross-machine communication. It is widely used when there has to be an exchange of data between applications, even when they are written on two completely different platforms or in different languages.

- **Custom XML**: Same as above, where you might have your own XML format and not use any defined methods.

Ditto and XML formats

To allow Ditto to present the aggregated data as XML, you must keep the following points in mind:

- The document must be created with the content type as **text/xml**, which can be changed under the **Page Settings** tab of the Document page.

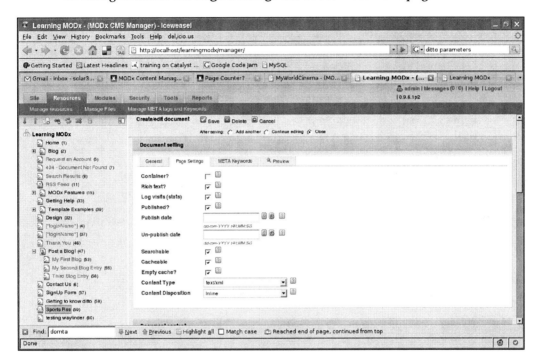

- The template must be selected as blank
- The content must be a call to Ditto, and must have an &format parameter with the format being one of the following:
    ◦ HTML
    ◦ JSON
    ◦ XML
    ◦ Atom
    ◦ RSS

Creating RSS views for each category

Now that we have categories and understand about aggregation and XML formats, let's create three documents that will display the latest blogs added from a single category. Create three documents with the following details:

Document 1:

Field Name	Value
Title	**Sports RSS**
Use Template	(Blank)
Content	[!Ditto? &parents=`47` &filter=`tvBlogc ategories,Sports,7` &format=`rss`!]
Content Type	text/xml
Parent	58 (The ID of your document — Getting to know ditto)

Document 2:

Field Name	Value
Title	**Lifestyle RSS**
Use Template	(Blank)
Content	[!Ditto? &parents=`47` &filter=`tvBlogc ategories,Lifestyle,7` &format=`rss`!]
Content Type	text/xml
Parent	58 (The ID of your document — Getting to know ditto)

Document 3:

Field Name	Value
Title	**IT Rss**
Use Template	(Blank)
Content	[!Ditto? &parents=`47` &filter=`tvBlogc ategories,IT,7` &format=`rss`!]
Content Type	text/xml
Parent	58 (The ID of your document — Getting to know ditto)

Now preview the pages and you will see something like the following:

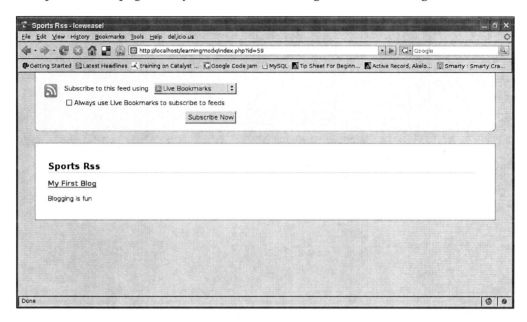

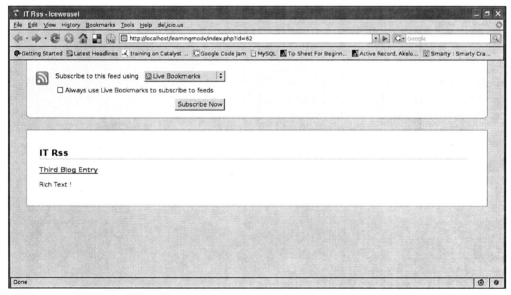

As you can see, each document only lists the aggregation of blogs for a single category. Also notice a different icon in the document tree. This indicates that the document is an XML document:

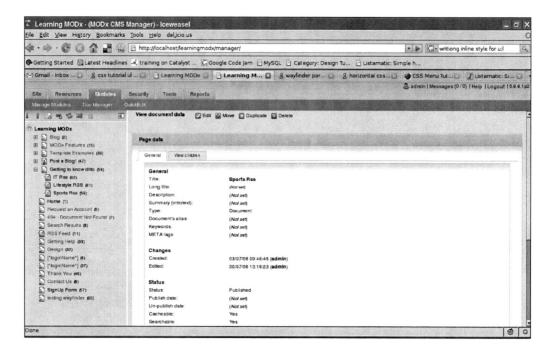

All the snippet calls in the previous document use parameters that we have already learned, except for the filter parameter which is explained below.

Filtering

Ditto allows you to filter certain documents from being aggregated, based on filtering rules that you define. These rules are passed as a value to the parameter &filter. The general format of the filtering rules is:

```
Field,criterion,mode
```

where:

- Field is any field from the document, like the ID or title; it can also be a template variable. If the field is a template variable, the field name must be prefixed with tv.
- criterion is any value with which you want to compare the field's value.
- mode is a number that defines what kind of operation has to be performed.

The following is a list of all the operations possible:

Filter	Mode
is not equal to the criterion (!=)	1
is equal to the criterion (==)	2
is less than the criterion (<)	3
is greater than the criterion (>)	4
is less than or equal to the criterion (<=)	5
is greater than or equal to the criterion (>=)	6
does not contain the text of the criterion	7
does contain the text of the criterion	8

For example, if you want to filter a document with ID 2, you would write:

    id,2,1

Here, each such rule is called a clause. `id,2,1` forms a clause.

Multiple clauses

You can also have multiple filtering clauses by separating each clause with a |
symbol. The | behaves like the or operator. If any one of the conditions is true,
then the document is filtered.

For example, you may want to filter the documents with an ID that is less than 4 and
greater than 100.

The clause for filtering the documents less than ID 4 would be:

    id,4,3

From the above table, mode 3 stands for "is less than the criterion". The clause means
that you should use `id` as the criterion, and filter the documents that have the value
for the criterion (`id`) as less than 4.

The clause for filtering the documents greater than ID 100 would be:

    id,100,4

As from the above table, mode 4 stands for "is greater than the criterion". So, the rule
to filter out documents for any of the above conditions would be:

    id,4,3 | id,100,4

And the whole expression to Ditto would be:

    [!ditto? &someparametere... &filter=`id,4,3 | id,100,4`!]

Extenders

Ditto also allows developers to extend the functionality of Ditto with new snippets that depend on Ditto. Such snippets are called extenders. There are a few Ditto extender snippets that were included in the installation of MODx. When you want to use an extender, you must tell Ditto which snippet to use by passing the name of the extender as an argument to the `&extenders` parameter.

Summary

In this chapter, you have learned about one very useful snippet called Ditto. You have seen how to create aggregation and feeds, and how to create feeds for separate categories. You have also learned about tagging and how to tag documents and use them in MODx.

Creating Lists

MODx allows menus to be dynamically created, based on the content available, as documents. Menus are basically a list of documents, and submenus are a list of lists (list within a menu list). In MODx, the simplest way to create lists of all the documents from the nested tables to the simple lines of text is with the use of the [[wayfinder]] snippet. In this chapter, we will learn how MODx allows us to create these lists dynamically, and also learn how to present them as menus.

Menu details in document properties

Every document that can be shown in a menu must have the **Shown in Menu** option enabled in the document's setting page. The **Document setting** page also has two other options related to menus:

- **Menu title** — what to show in the menu. The document title is used instead, if this value is left blank.

- **Menu index** — when a list of the documents that are to be listed in the menu is created, the menu index can be used to sort the documents in the required order. Menu index is a number and, when creating lists, we can specify how we want to use the index.

Authentication and authorization

When creating the list of documents, **WayFinder** lists only those documents that are accessible by the user depending on the access permissions set for each document and the web user group to which the user belongs. For more information on access permissions, refer to the previous chapter on *Authentication and Authorization* (Chapter 5).

Getting to know WayFinder

WayFinder is a snippet that outputs the structure of the documents as reflected in the document tree. It creates the lists of all the documents that can be accessed by the current user, and those that have been marked as **Shown in Menu** in the document properties. Let's try out an exercise to discover WayFinder.

1. Create a new document
2. Set the name as **testing wayfinder**
3. Choose the template as **Empty**
4. Place the following as the content:

   - `[[Wayfinder?startId=`0` ]]`

5. Save the document and preview it

You will see a screen like the following:

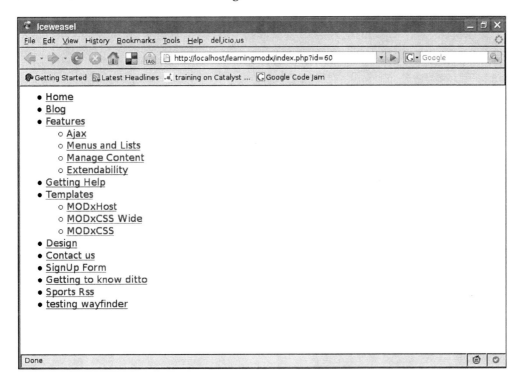

Notice that it has created a list of all the documents, even the ones from the sample site. And each item is a link, so clicking on it leads you to the corresponding document. The generated HTML will look like the following:

```
<ul><li><a href="http://localhost/learningMODx/" title="Home"
                                        >Home</a></li>
<li><a href="/learningMODx/index.php?id=2" title="Blog"
                                        >Blog</a></li>
<li><a href="/learningMODx/index.php?id=15" title="MODx Features"
>Features</a><ul><li><a href="/learningMODx/index.php?id=16"
title="Ajax" >Ajax</a></li>
<li><a href="/learningMODx/index.php?id=22" title="Menus and Lists"
                                        >Menus and Lists</a></li>
<li><a href="/learningMODx/index.php?id=14" title="Content
                    Management" >Manage Content</a></li>
<li class="last"><a href="/learningMODx/index.php?id=24"
    title="Extendable by design" >Extendability</a></li>
</ul></li>
<li><a href="/learningMODx/index.php?id=33" title="Getting Help"
                                        >Getting Help</a></li>
```

```
<li><a href="/learningMODx/index.php?id=39" title="Template Examples"
>Templates</a><ul><li><a href="index.php?id=39" title="MODxHost"
>MODxHost</a></li>
<li><a href="/learningMODx/index.php?id=42" title="MODxCSS Wide"
                                    >MODxCSS Wide</a></li>
<li class="last"><a href="/learningMODx/index.php?id=43"
                title="MODxCSS" >MODxCSS</a></li>
</ul></li>
<li><a href="/learningMODx/index.php?id=32" title="Design"
                        >Design</a></li>
<li><a href="/learningMODx/index.php?id=6" title="Contact Us"
                        >Contact us</a></li>
<li><a href="/learningMODx/index.php?id=57" title="SignUp Form"
                        >SignUp Form</a></li>
<li><a href="/learningMODx/index.php?id=58" title="Getting to know
                    ditto" >Getting to know ditto</a></li>
<li><a href="/learningMODx/index.php?id=59" title="Sports Rss"
                        >Sports Rss</a></li>
<li class="last active"><a href="/learningMODx/index.php?id=60"
        title="testing wayfinder" >testing wayfinder</a></li>
</ul>
```

As can be seen above, the generated list is just a set of `<ul>` and `<li>` tags. Let's go step by step in understanding how the above output can be customized and themed, starting with menus of one level.

Theming

To be able to theme the list generated by WayFinder to appear as menus, we need to understand how WayFinder works in more detail. In this section, we will show you step by step how to create a simple menu without any sub-items, and then proceed to creating menus with sub-items.

Creating a simple menu

Since, for now, we only want a menu without any submenu item, we have to show documents only from the top level of the document tree. By default, WayFinder will reflect the complete structure of the document tree, including the documents within containers as seen in the preceding screenshot. WayFinder lets you choose the depth of the list with the `&level` parameter. `&level` takes a value indicating the number of levels that WayFinder should include in the menu. For our example, since we only want a simple menu with no submenu items, `&level` is 1.

Now let us change the `testing wayfinder` document, which we just created, to the following code:

```
[[Wayfinder?startId=`0` &level=`1` ]]
```

Preview the document now, and you will see that the source code of the generated page in place of `Wayfinder` is:

```
<ul><li><a href="http://localhost/learningMODx/" title="Home"
                                    >Home</a></li>
<li><a href="/learningMODx/index.php?id=2" title="Blog"
                                    >Blog</a></li>
<li><a href="/learningMODx/index.php?id=15" title="MODx Features"
                                    >Features</a></li>
<li><a href="/learningMODx/index.php?id=33" title="Getting Help"
                                    >Getting Help</a></li>
<li><a href="/learningMODx/index.php?id=39" title="Template Examples"
                                    >Templates</a></li>
<li><a href="/learningMODx/index.php?id=32" title="Design"
                                    >Design</a></li>
<li><a href="/learningMODx/index.php?id=6" title="Contact Us"
                                    >Contact us</a></li>
<li><a href="/learningMODx/index.php?id=57" title="SignUp Form"
                                    >SignUp Form</a></li>
<li><a href="/learningMODx/index.php?id=58" title="Getting to know
                    ditto" >Getting to know ditto</a></li>
<li><a href="/learningMODx/index.php?id=59" title="Sports Rss"
                                    >Sports Rss</a></li>
<li class="last active"><a href="/learningMODx/index.php?id=60"
        title="testing wayfinder" >testing wayfinder</a></li>
</ul>
```

Now, if we can just give `<ul>` and `<li>` respective classes, we can style them to appear as a menu. We can do this by passing the class names to the parameter `&rowClass`.

Change the contents of the preceding `testing wayfinder` to:

```
<div id="menu">
[!Wayfinder?startId=`0` &level=`1` %rowClass=`menu`!]
</div>
```

Now, open `style.css` from the `root` folder, and change the CSS to the following. What we are doing is styling the preceding generated list to appear like a menu using CSS:

```
* { padding:2; margin:0; border:1; }
body { margin:0 20px; background:#8CEC81; }
#banner { background: #2BB81B; border-top:5px solid #8CEC81; border-
                                      bottom:5px solid #8CEC81; }
#banner h1 { padding:10px; }
#wrapper { background: #8CEC81; }
#container { width: 100%; background: #2BB81B; float: left; }
#content { background: #ffffff; height:600px; padding:0 10px 10px
                                      10px; clear:both; }
#footer { background: #2BB81B; border-top:5px solid #8CEC81; border-
                                      bottom:5px solid #8CEC81; }
.clearing { clear:both; height:0; }
#content #col-1 {float:left;width:500px; margin:0px;padding:0px;}
#content #col-2 {float:right; width:300px; margin:0px; padding:30px 0
           10px 25px; border-left:3px solid #99cc66; height:500px;}
#content #col-2 div {padding-bottom:20px;}

#menu {
background:#ffffff;
float: left;
}

#menu ul {
list-style: none;
margin: 0;
padding: 0;
width: 48em;
float: left;
}

#menu ul li {
display: inline;
}
#menu a, #menu h2 {
font: bold 11px/16px arial, helvetica, sans-serif;
display: inline;
border-width: 1px;
border-style: solid;
border-color: #ccc #888 #555 #bbb;
margin: 0;
```

```
padding: 2px 3px;
}

#menu h2 {
color: #fff;
background: #000;
text-transform: uppercase;
}

#menu a {
color: #000;
background: #2BB81B;
text-decoration: none;
}

#menu a:hover {
color: #2BB81B;
background: #fff;
}
```

Now preview the page and you will see something like the following:

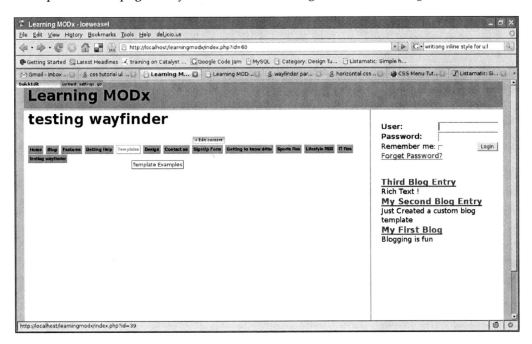

The HTML code returned will be similar to the following:

```
<ul><li class="menu"><a href="http://localhost/learningMODx/"
                                 title="Home" >Home</a></li>
<li class="menu"><a href="/learningMODx/index.php?id=2" title="Blog"
                                                    >Blog</a></li>
<li class="menu"><a href="/learningMODx/index.php?id=15" title="MODx
                                  Features" >Features</a></li>
<li class="menu"><a href="/learningMODx/index.php?id=33"
            title="Getting Help" >Getting Help</a></li>
<li class="menu"><a href="/learningMODx/index.php?id=39"
           title="Template Examples" >Templates</a></li>
<li class="menu"><a href="/learningMODx/index.php?id=32"
                        title="Design" >Design</a></li>
<li class="menu"><a href="/learningMODx/index.php?id=6"
                 title="Contact Us" >Contact us</a></li>
<li class="menu"><a href="/learningMODx/index.php?id=57"
                title="SignUp Form" >SignUp Form</a></li>
<li class="menu"><a href="/learningMODx/index.php?id=58" title=
         "Getting to know ditto" >Getting to know ditto</a></li>
<li class="menu"><a href="/learningMODx/index.php?id=59"
                  title="Sports Rss" >Sports Rss</a></li>
<li class="menu last active"><a href="/learningMODx/index.php?id=60"
            title="testing wayfinder" >testing wayfinder</a></li>
</ul>
```

Notice that for each menu item, the class menu has been applied. Though we have not applied any custom style to the menu class, we have shown you that when you are building more fine-grained menu systems, you have the ability to have every item associated with a class.

Nested menus

When we have more than one level of the menu structure, we will want different styling for the top menu and the menu items. This effectively means that we need to have different classes for different levels. Also, some menu systems have different styling for the first and the last elements. Such flexibility in styling is also possible with the WayFinder. Let us consider a two-level structure with the class names that we might want illustrated in the side. For this example, the list will be:

```
<ul>
  <li> Menu1 Name </li>                   outer first
    <ul>
      <li> Menu item 1</li>               inner first
      <li>Menu item 2</li>                inner
      <li>Menu item 3</li>                inner
```

```
        <li>Menu item 4</li>                          inner last
      </ul>
    <li> Menu2 Name</li>                               outer
      <ul>
        <li> Menu item 1</li>                          inner first
        <li>Menu item 2</li>                           inner
        <li>Menu item 3</li>                           inner
        <li>Menu item 4</li>                           inner last
      </ul>
    <li> Menu3 Name</li>                               outer last
      <ul>
        <li> Menu item 1</li>                          inner first
        <li>Menu item 2</li>                           inner
        <li>Menu item 3</li>                           inner
        <li>Menu item 4</li>                           inner last
      </ul>
  </ul>
```

The following are the list of parameters that we will need to use to be able to have the respective class names in the generated list:

Parameter	Definition
&firstClass	CSS class denoting the first item at a given menu level
&lastClass	CSS class denoting the last item at a given menu level
&hereClass	CSS class denoting the "you are here" state, all the way up to the chain
&selfClass	CSS class denoting the "you are here" state, for only the current doc
&parentClass	CSS class denoting that the menu item is a folder (has children)
&rowClass	CSS class denoting each output row
&levelClass	CSS class denoting each output row's level; the level number will be added to the specified class (that is, level1, level2, level3, and so on)
&outerClass	CSS class for the outer template
&innerClass	CSS class for the inner template
&webLinkClass	CSS class for weblinks

Now change the content in the testing wayfinder document to:

```
<div id="menu">
[Wayfinder?startId=`0` &level=`2` &outerClass=`outer`
&innerClass='inner' &lastClass=`last` &firstClass=`first`
&hereClass=`active`!]
</div>
```

This code will result in an output similar to the following. Notice that the class names are similar to the structure that we wanted as outlined earlier.

```
<div id="menu">
<ul class="outer"><li class="first"><a href="http://localhost/
learningMODx/" title="Home" >Home</a></li>
<li><a href="/learningMODx/index.php?id=2" title="Blog"
                                        >Blog</a></li>
<li><a href="/learningMODx/index.php?id=15" title="MODx Features"
>Features</a><ul class="'inner' "><li class="first"><a href="/
learningMODx/index.php?id=16" title="Ajax" >Ajax</a></li>
<li><a href="/learningMODx/index.php?id=22" title="Menus and Lists"
                                        >Menus and Lists</a></li>
<li><a href="/learningMODx/index.php?id=14" title="Content
                    Management" >Manage Content</a></li>
<li class="last"><a href="/learningMODx/index.php?id=24"
    title="Extendable by design" >Extendability</a></li>
</ul></li>
<li><a href="/learningMODx/index.php?id=33" title="Getting Help"
                                        >Getting Help</a></li>
<li><a href="/learningMODx/index.php?id=39" title="Template Examples"
>Templates</a><ul class="'inner' "><li class="first"><a href="index.
php?id=39" title="MODxHost" >MODxHost</a></li>
<li><a href="/learningMODx/index.php?id=42" title="MODxCSS Wide"
                                        >MODxCSS Wide</a></li>
<li class="last"><a href="/learningMODx/index.php?id=43"
                    title="MODxCSS" >MODxCSS</a></li>
</ul></li>
<li><a href="/learningMODx/index.php?id=32" title="Design"
                                        >Design</a></li>
<li><a href="/learningMODx/index.php?id=6" title="Contact Us"
                                        >Contact us</a></li>
<li><a href="/learningMODx/index.php?id=57" title="SignUp Form"
                                        >SignUp Form</a></li>
<li><a href="/learningMODx/index.php?id=58" title="Getting to know
                            ditto" >Getting to know ditto</a></li>
<li><a href="/learningMODx/index.php?id=59" title="Sports Rss"
                                        >Sports Rss</a></li>
<li><a href="/learningMODx/index.php?id=61" title="Lifestyle RSS"
                                        >Lifestyle RSS</a></li>
<li><a href="/learningMODx/index.php?id=62" title="IT Rss" >IT
                                        Rss</a></li>
<li class="last active"><a href="/learningMODx/index.php?id=60"
        title="testing wayfinder" >testing wayfinder</a></li>
</ul>
</div>
```

Now preview the page and it will look like the following:

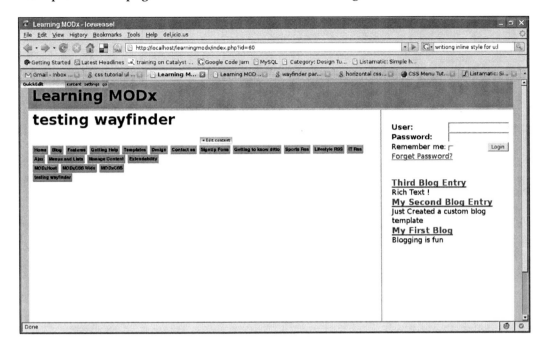

Notice that the inner items are also shown. We will change this behavior by adding some CSS styling to show this inner menu only on hover.

Now, edit `style.css` to the following:

```
* { padding:2; margin:0; border:1; }
body { margin:0 20px; background:#8CEC81; }
#banner { background: #2BB81B; border-top:5px solid #8CEC81; border-
                                  bottom:5px solid #8CEC81; }
#banner h1 { padding:10px; }
#wrapper { background: #8CEC81; }
#container { width: 100%; background: #2BB81B; float: left; }
#content { background: #ffffff; height:600px; padding:0 10px 10px
                                  10px; clear:both; }
#footer { background: #2BB81B; border-top:5px solid #8CEC81; border-
                                  bottom:5px solid #8CEC81; }
.clearing { clear:both; height:0; }
#content #col-1 {float:left;width:500px; margin:0px;padding:0px;}
#content #col-2 {float:right; width:300px; margin:0px; padding:30px 0
          10px 25px; border-left:3px solid #99cc66; height:500px;}
#content #col-2 div {padding-bottom:20px;}
#menu {
```

```
background:#ffffff;
float: left;
}

#menu ul {
list-style: none;
margin: 0;
padding: 0;
width: 48em;
float: left;
}

#menu ul li {
display: inline;
}

#menu a, #menu h2 {
font: bold 11px/16px arial, helvetica, sans-serif;
display: inline;
border-width: 1px;
border-style: solid;
border-color: #ccc #888 #555 #bbb;
margin: 0;
padding: 2px 3px;
}

#menu h2 {
color: #fff;
background: #000;
text-transform: uppercase;
}

#menu a {
color: #000;
background: #2BB81B;
text-decoration: none;
}

#menu a:hover {
color: #2BB81B;
background: #fff;
}

#menu li {position: relative;}

#menu ul ul {
position: relative;
z-index: 500;
}
```

```
#menu ul ul ul {
top: 0;
left: 100%;
}
div#menu ul ul,
div#menu ul li:hover ul ul,
div#menu ul ul li:hover ul ul
{display: none;}
div#menu ul li:hover ul,
div#menu ul ul li:hover ul,
div#menu ul ul ul li:hover ul
{display: block;}
```

Now preview the page; it will look like the following, with submenu items on hover working fine.

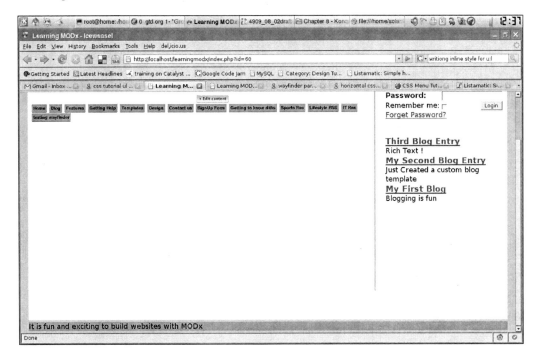

Note again that the class name generated above is only for informative purpose, to have a finer-grained menu system when you need it. Had you replaced the call to Wayfinder with [!Wayfinder?startId=`0` &level=`2`!], it would have still worked.

Now that we have the menus appearing in this page, let us make them appear in all the pages. Note that we created this page only for testing, and to find out how WayFinder works. We will need to use the code we have come up with in this page in the default Learning MODx template.

Change the default Learning MODx template to the following:

```
<!DOCTYPE html PUBLIC "-//W3C//DTD XHTML 1.1//EN" "http://www.w3.org/
TR/xhtml11/DTD/xhtml11.dtd"> <html xmlns="http://www.w3.org/1999/
xhtml" xml:lang="en">
  <head>
    <title>Learning MODx</title>
    <meta http-equiv="Content-Type" content="text/html; charset=iso-
                                                        8859-1" />
    <link rel="stylesheet" type="text/css" href="style.css" />
  </head>
  <body>
    <div id="banner">
      <h1>Learning MODx</h1>
    </div>

    <div id="wrapper">
      <div id="container">
  <div id="content">
    <div id="col-1">
        <div id="menu">
          [!Wayfinder?startId=`0` &level=`2` &outerClass=`outer`
&innerClass='inner' &lastClass=`last` &firstClass=`first`
&hereClass=`active`!]
        </div>
        <h1>[*pagetitle*]</h1>
        <br/>
        [*#content*]
      </div>
      <div id="col-2">
        <div > [!WebLogin!] </div>
          <div>
            [!Ditto? &parents=`47` &tpl=`dittofrontpage`!]
          </div>
      </div>
    </div>
  </div>
        </div>
        <div class="clearing"> </div>
      </div> <!-- end of wrapper div -->
      <div id="footer">It is fun and exciting to build websites with
                                        MODx</div></body>
  </html>
```

Save the template and preview the Home Page. It will look like the following:

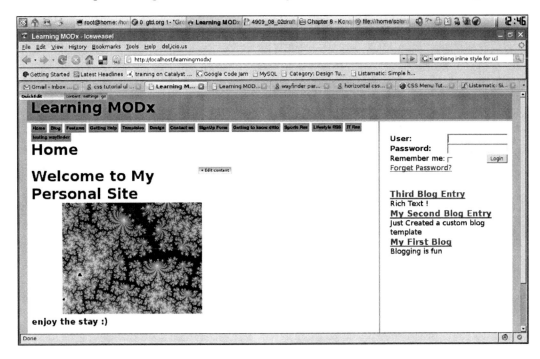

Now that you have learned how to theme lists that are two-levels deep, you may be wondering how to theme lists that are more than two-levels deep. You can theme such lists using the `levelClass` parameter. For example, if you set `&levelClass = `level``, then the level items will have the classes `level1`, `level2`, `level3`.

Changing the name in the menu

Let us change the name of the menu title for the page called 'Getting to know ditto', which lists all the blog entries in RSS format that we created in the previous chapter when we learned about tags. Let us give it a different name for the menu. To do that, perform the following steps:

1. Click on the document and edit.
2. Change the menu title to **Feeds**.
3. Save the document.
4. Repeat the above steps for the document **SignUp Form** and change the menu name to **Register**.

Doc Manager

Doc Manager is a module that allows you to change the template, template variables, and other document properties of one or more documents. Using the Doc Manager makes it easier to make changes to multiple documents simultaneously. Doc Manager can be accessed from the **Doc Manager** menu item in the **Modules** menu. The following is a screenshot of the Doc Manager:

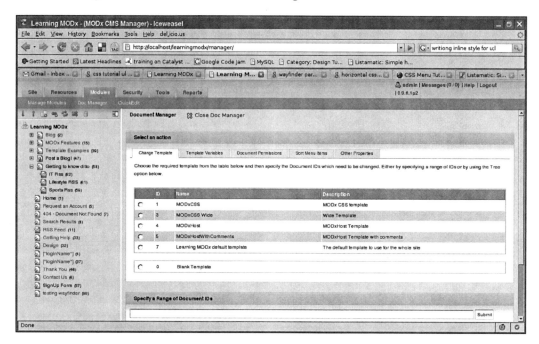

As you can see, it has five tabs:

Tab Name	Functionality
Change Template	Change the template of one or more documents
Template Variables	Change the values in the template variables for one or more documents
Document Permissions	Add or remove one or more documents to or from a document group
Sort Menu Items	Provides a drag-and-drop menu ordering functionality for the child documents of a selected parent
Other Properties	Set document dates, authors, and other Yes/No options such as cacheable, published, and so on, for one or more documents

The following is the screenshot of **Sort Menu Items** after selecting the **Parent** as
`Learning MODx` (root folder) by clicking on it.

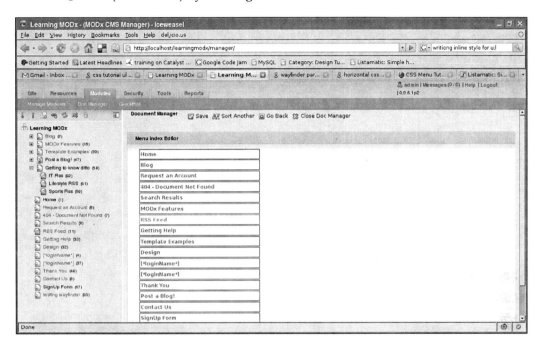

Except for **Sort Menu Items**, all the other actions have a field in the bottom called
Specify a Range of Document IDs. The documents on which the changes have to
be made are selected by entering the appropriate value in this field. You can specify
a single document, or a range of documents, with the – operator. You can specify a
document and all its immediate children by entering the document ID followed by
an *. You can specify a document and all its children by entering the document ID
followed by **. You can have a list of all these syntaxes separated by commas; for
example: 10,20-30,5*,8**. This will make the selected changes in:

- Document 10
- Document 20 to document 30
- Document 5 and all its immediate children
- Document 8 and all its children

Removing pages from the menu

You might notice that menu items are generated even for the pages from the MODx sample site. Since our purpose for having these pages is only to look at them and learn, we do not want them to be appearing in our menus. Also, there are a few pages that we have created to test the functionalities; we will hide them too. You can hide the documents one by one by selecting the document, clicking on **Edit**, un-checking the **Shown in Menu** checkbox, and saving the document. Alternatively, you can use the Doc Manager to change the properties for a set of documents.

To change the **Shown in Menu** setting using the Doc Manager:

1. Click on the **Modules** menu and the **Doc Manager** menu item.
2. Click on the **Other Properties** tab in the right content area.
3. Change **Available Settings** to **Show/Hide in Menu**.
4. Select the **Hide in Menu** checkbox.
5. In **Specify a Range of Document IDs**, list the IDs for all the documents that you want to hide separated by commas. It can be something like 2*,15*,33,39*,32,6,60. Notice that * stands for the document with the given ID and its immediate children.

Note that the above ID list could be different for you depending on the order you created the documents.

Now click on **Preview** and the page will look like the following:

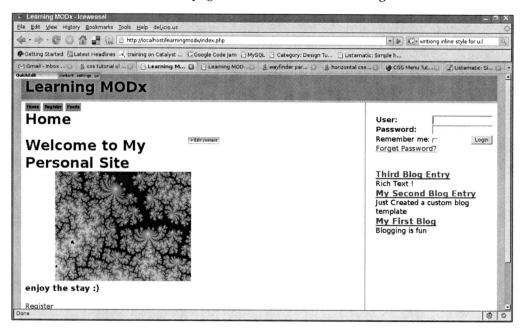

More theming using chunks

Now that we have learned how to give custom class names for generated `<ul>` `<li>` unordered lists, we are able to theme them by having the corresponding styles for the classes. What if we wanted to have a list that is not a `<ul>` `<li>` type? Or what if we wanted to have more control over how the list is generated? WayFinder also allows the user to customize the structure of the generated lists, using chunks. Similar to the use of custom classes, MODx has separate parameters that specify which chunk to use for which level and so on. As with any chunk, the dynamic content comes from the available placeholders that are set by the snippet, which in our case is WayFinder. In this section, we will look at breadcrumbs and discuss those parameters pertaining to templates that are used for creating the breadcrumb trail.

Breadcrumb navigation

Breadcrumbs are those small links that you generally see in the top of a page that help you to understand which part of the site you are in and how you got there.

For example, if you are accessing a blog entry inside a `blog` folder, then the breadcrumb would be:

```
home>>blog>>blogname
```

In the above example, `home` and `blog` are links to take you to the roots of the current document.

The following is the code and the explanation of how breadcrumbs can be created in MODx using WayFinder.

```
<a href="/" title="Home">Home</a> &raquo; [!Wayfinder? &startId=`0`
&outerTpl=`BreadCrumbOuter` &rowTpl=`BreadCrumbRow` &activeParentRowTp
l=`BreadCrumbActiveParentRow` &hereTpl=`BreadCrumbHere`!]
```

`&raquo` gets converted to >>. The above call to `Wayfinder` uses different chunks for different levels to process and create the list. Overleaf is an explanation for each template parameter and what the chunk should contain. It will be easier to understand the wrapper placeholders if you remember the following concepts:

- The call to `WayFinder` generates document lists based on the given parameters.
- For each document in the document list, the respective placeholders in the appropriate chunk are replaced by the content of the document. The chunks being used are determined from the value of the corresponding snippet parameter. The innermost document list is generated first and then the outermost document list.

Parameter	Given Chunk Name	For what items the chunk will be called	Code for the chunk	Explanation of the code
&outertpl	BreadCrumbOuter	When processing the outmost container. (What it should be instead of `<ul></ul>` for the outermost level.)	`[+wf.wrapper+]`	The template variable `[+wf.wrapper+]` specifies where the innermost content will be inserted.
&rowTpl	BreadCrumbrow	When processing each document in the document list. (What it should be instead of `<li></li>` for every level.)		We leave it empty, as for the breadcrumb, we want only the current item and the parent item of the current item to be shown.
ActiveParentRowTpl	BreadCrumbActiveParentRow	When processing the parent document of the current document.	`<a href="[+wf.link+]" title="[+wf.title+]">[+wf.linktext+]</a> &raquo; [+wf.wrapper+]`	We display a link for the parent document using the placeholders for link, title, and linktext. And then we specify where the inner contents should be inserted. (If it is a parent document, it definitely has at least the current document as the inner level document.)
&hereTpl	BreadCrumbHere	When processing the current document.	`[+wf.linktext+]`	We just show the current document's menu title here, as we do not want a link to the document when we are already in that page.

Multiple calls

It is possible to have *multiple calls* to WayFinder within the same document or template. This might be necessary when you want to have multiple menu systems in the same page. For instance, you might want to have a primary menu at the top and additional menus on the left or right. You can have one call to WayFinder for the menus, one for the breadcrumb trail, and so on. To do this, you will only have to place the corresponding WayFinder snippet calls at the appropriate positions in the template being used.

Example structure:

```
HTML

    <!-- WayFinder snippet call for breadcrumbs -->
<a href="/" title="Home">Home</a> &raquo; [!Wayfinder? &startId=`0`
&outerTpl=`BreadCrumbOuter` &rowTpl=`BreadCrumbRow` &activeParentRowTp
l=`BreadCrumbActiveParentRow` &hereTpl=`BreadCrumbHere

HTML

    <!-- WayFinder snippet  call for menu ->
[!Wayfinder?startId=`0` &level=`2` &outerClass=`outer`
&innerClass='inner' &lastClass=`last` &firstClass=`first`
&hereClass=`active`!]
```

Summary

We have learned how to use the snippet `[[WayFinder]]` to create lists of documents. We also saw the usage of parameters in WayFinder to make the list creation flexible. All WayFinder parameters help in doing one of the following three actions:

- Filtering— to what list?
- Styling—which style classes do I use?
- Structuring—which chunk defines my template?

We have seen examples for filtering, styling, and structuring. In the process, we have also added a menu system for our site. We have also learned how to use the Doc Manager module to change the properties for a group of documents quickly, without having to do them one by one.

8
Snippets

We have been using snippets all this while without many details on what they actually are. In this chapter, you will learn more about snippets. We will explore the snippets that come with MODx and those that are available for download. You will learn how to install a snippet, use a snippet, and navigate its custom functionalities. As an example, we will be looking at one snippet called Jot and the process of allowing comments on posts.

Working of snippets

Snippets are units of code that can be called from a document or a template.

A snippet can do the following three things:

- Return text or HTML
- Populate template variables
- Process a chunk and return its value

Almost anything that can be done in PHP can be done using a snippet. But how you control the output and flexibility of the snippet depends on how you use the snippet, to do one of the above activities or a combination of them.

A snippet can be called using one of the following notations:

- `[[snippetname]]` — cached call
- `[!snippetname!]` — non-cached call

In a cached call, a snippet is processed once, and whatever it generates is cached and used till the cache is cleared. But if the page in which the snippet is executed is not cached, the snippet will be processed anyway for every request. This may be useful for optimization in situations where the expected output from the snippet does not change frequently.

In a non-cached call, a snippet is processed each time the page loads. Hence, there is no cache optimization for speed for the snippet alone. This may be necessary for snippets interacting with forms where the processed output is going to be dynamic every time. Also, a page can be cached and only the snippet can be non-cached. This way the optimization for the whole page is still retained. All this is explained in more detail in Chapter 5.

Finding snippets

Whenever you want to add a new functionality to the site, the first step is to find the right snippet that can provide the site with such functionality. There are a few snippets that come packaged with MODx, in which case you don't have to install them. We will see one example of such a snippet in this section. In a later section of the chapter, you will learn how to install new snippets.

Now, let us consider how to add comments to blog entries. Searching in Google for 'MODx comments' brings the page `http://wiki.MODxcms.com/index.php/Jot` as one of the first links. This page shows us that Jot is a snippet that can be used for adding comments to blogs. Note that in this case, I have listed the name of the snippet. But there are literally hundreds of snippets, and the list of contributed snippets is growing rapidly. So, it is really necessary that you learn how to search for the right snippet that will get you what you want. You might also want to search for the snippets in the MODx repository or MODx forums

Learning about snippets

Now we have identified that we want to use the Jot snippet. What next?

- Try out the snippet with the minimal configuration.
- Check the list of available parameters.
- Use placeholders if it involves HTML that can be processed from a chunk.

An explanation for each of the preceding points follows. Note that this section is not specifically about Jot, but rather about learning how to use a new snippet.

Jot with the minimal configuration

Whenever you want to learn how to use a snippet, it is a good idea to try it out with the most minimal configuration needed. This way, you can be sure that your understanding of what the snippet does is correct. Reading through the page that we have just found (wiki documentation), it doesn't seem like there are any required parameters, and all parameters seem optional. So let us just go and place the Jot call below the posts in the blog template.

Edit the Learning MODx blog template and add the highlighted call to Jot, so that the template code looks like the following:

```
<!DOCTYPE html PUBLIC "-//W3C//DTD XHTML 1.1//EN" "http://www.w3.org/
TR/xhtml11/DTD/xhtml11.dtd"> <html xmlns="http://www.w3.org/1999/
xhtml" xml:lang="en">
 <head>
  <title>Learning MODx</title>
  <meta http-equiv="Content-Type" content="text/html; charset=iso-
                                                8859-1" />
  <link rel="stylesheet" type="text/css" href="style.css" />
 </head>
 <body>
  <div id="banner">
   <h1>Learning MODx</h1>
  </div>

  <div id="wrapper">
   <div id="container">
   <div id="content">
    <div id="col-1">
<div id="menu">
[!Wayfinder?startId=`0` &amp;level=`2` &amp;outerClass=`outer`
&amp;innerClass='inner' &amp;lastClass=`last` &amp;firstClass=`first`
&amp;hereClass=`active`!]
</div>
      <h1>[*pagetitle*]</h1>
      <br/>

      [*#content*]
      <br/>
    [!Jot!]
     </div>

     <div id="col-2">
     <div > [!WebLogin!] </div>

      <div>
      [!Ditto? &parents=`47` &tpl=`dittofrontpage`!]
      </div>
      </div>
    </div>
    </div>
    <div class="clearing"> </div>
   </div> <!-- end of wrapper div -->
   <div id="footer">It is fun and exciting to build websites with
                                      MODx</div></body>
 </html>
```

Now preview any of the posted blogs and it will look like the following:

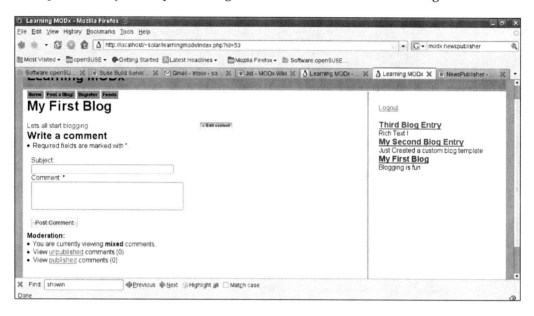

To change the default form, we have to find the parameter for the snippet with which we can specify the chunk to use. Then we need to learn which placeholders can be used in the chunk. Let's test if Jot is actually working by posting a comment. The following is a screenshot of how it looks after posting a comment.

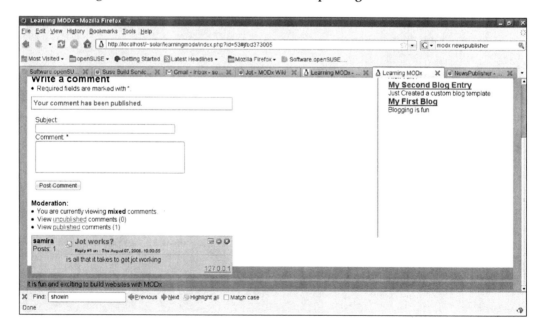

Note that some snippets vary their functionality based on whether you are logged in as a manager or not. Log out from the Manager interface, refresh the page and it will appear like the following:

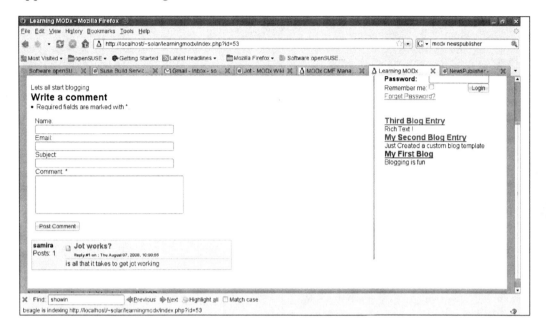

Snippet parameters

Snippet parameters, as you have already learned, are what allows you to control the functionality of a snippet. A parameter takes one or more value after the = sign. The parameter itself is preceded by an &.

Now, have a look at the available Jot parameters from the web page given earlier. We want to configure the behavior of Jot in two ways, and hence we need to identify the appropriate parameters to configure it.

- Restrict comments to authenticated users — &canpost
- Theme the comment form — &tplForm

The value that has to be passed to &tplForm is the name of the HTML chunk to be used for the form. &canpost takes a comma-separated list of the names of groups that are allowed to post the comments. Now let us change the highlighted call to Jot, in the preceding code of the Learning MODx blog template, to the following:

```
[!Jot? &canpost=`Registered Users`!]
```

Now log out of the Web interface, log out of the Manager interface, and preview the blog page. It will appear like the following:

You won't see the comment form. This is because of the preceding call where we specified to only allow registered users to see the comment form by assigning `&canpost=`Registered Users` ` in the Jot snippet call.

Now log in through the Web interface as samira, the user you created in a previous chapter, and the page looks like the following:

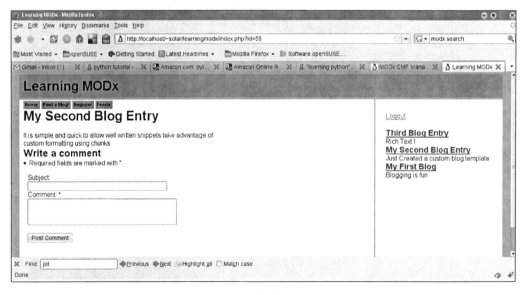

As you can see, the comments form is available.

Now that we have achieved the first of our two objectives (to restrict comments to registered users), let's get started with the second objective (theming the comment form). First, we need to specify which chunk to use as the custom form. For this, modify the preceding call to Jot to the following.

```
[!Jot? &tplForm=`comments` &canpost=`Registered Users`!]
```

Preview any comment page and it should look like the following:

Notice that instead of the comments form, we see the static text comments. This is because Jot was unable to find the chunk named comments. Now, just for demonstrational purposes, let us create a chunk with the following details:

Field Name	Value
Name	comments
Content	Testing the comment form
Category	Learning MODx

If you preview the page now, it will look like the following:

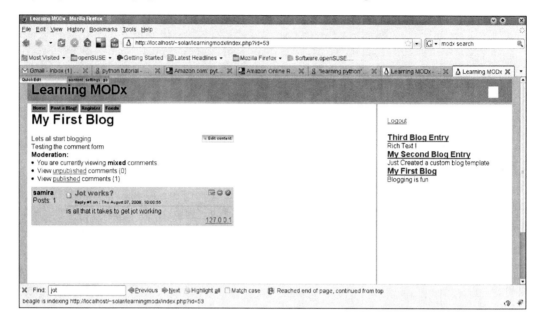

As you can see, the static text from the chunk comments "Testing the comment form" has been replaced over here. Now, instead of this static text, what we require is a form that Jot can understand. In the case of Jot, there is not any documentation, as of writing this chapter, on how to write a form chunk for Jot. When you come across situations like this, you can understand what a snippet expects in a custom form by opening its own default templates. The wiki documentation states that the default templates are in the `jot/template` directory. The next section has more details on this. For now, just understand that we are opening a file `chunk.form.inc.html` from `assests/snippets/jot/templates/`, which has the following code:

```
<a name="jf[+jot.link.id+]"></a>
<h2>[+form.edit:is=`1`:then=`Edit comment`:else=`Write a
                                    comment`+]</h2>
<div class="jot-list">
<ul>
 <li>Required fields are marked with <b>*</b>.
</ul>
</div>
[+form.error:isnt=`0`:then=`
<div class="jot-err">
[+form.error:select=`
&-3=You are trying to re-submit the same post. You have probably
                    clicked the submit button more than once.
```

```
&-2=Your comment has been rejected.
&-1=Your comment has been saved, it will first be reviewed before it
                                              is published.
&1=You are trying to re-submit the same post. You have probably
                    clicked the submit button more than once.
&2=The security code you entered was incorrect.
&3=You can only post once each [+jot.postdelay+] seconds.
&4=Your comment has been rejected.
&5=[+form.errormsg:ifempty=`You didn't enter all the required
                                              fields`+]
`+]
</div>
`:strip+]
[+form.confirm:isnt=`0`:then=`
<div class="jot-cfm">
[+form.confirm:select=`
&1=Your comment has been published.
&2=Your comment has been saved, it will first be reviewed before it
                                              is published.
&3=Comment saved.
`+]
</div>
`:strip+]
<form method="post" action="[+form.action:esc+]#jf[+jot.link.id+]"
                                              class="jot-form">
    <fieldset>
    <input name="JotForm" type="hidden" value="[+jot.id+]" />
    <input name="JotNow" type="hidden" value="[+jot.seed+]" />
    <input name="parent" type="hidden" value="[+form.field.parent+]"
                                                              />

    [+form.moderation:is=`1`:then=`
        <div class="jot-row">
            <b>Created on:</b> [+form.field.createdon:date=`%a %B %d,
                                              %Y at %H:%M`+]<br />
            <b>Created by:</b> [+form.field.createdby:userinfo=
                `username`:ifempty=`[+jot.guestname+]`+]<br />
            <b>IP address:</b> [+form.field.secip+]<br />
            <b>Published:</b> [+form.field.published:
                        select=`0=No&1=Yes`+]<br />
            [+form.field.publishedon:gt=`0`:then=`
                <b>Published on:</b> [+form.field.publishedon:date=`%a
                                    %B %d, %Y at %H:%M`+]<br />
                <b>Published by:</b> [+form.field.publishedby:
userinfo=`username`:ifempty=` - `+]<br />
`+]
                [+form.field.editedon:gt=`0`:then=`
```

```
                   <b>Edited on:</b> [+form.field.editedon:date=`%a %B %d,
                                              %Y at %H:%M`+]<br />
                   <b>Edited by:</b> [+form.field.editedby:
userinfo=`username`:ifempty=` -`+]<br />
`+]
        </div>
    `:strip+]

    [+form.guest:is=`1`:then=`
        <label for="name">Name:<br />
    <input tabindex="[+jot.seed:math=`?+1`+]" name="name" type="text"
                size="40" value="[+form.field.custom.name:esc+]" />
        </label>
        <label for="email">Email:<br />
        <input tabindex="[+jot.seed:math=`?+2`+]" name="email"
type="text" size="40" value="[+form.field.custom.email:esc+]" />
        </label>
    `:strip+]

    <label for="title">Subject:<br />
    <input tabindex="[+jot.seed:math=`?+3`+]" name="title" type="text"
                      size="40" value="[+form.field.title:esc+]" />
    </label>
    <label for="content">Comment: *<br />
    <textarea tabindex="[+jot.seed:math=`?+4`+]" name="content"
       cols="50" rows="8">[+form.field.content:esc+]</textarea>
    </label><br />

 [+jot.captcha:is=`1`:then=`
        <div style="width:150px;margin-top: 5px;margin-bottom: 5px;"><a
href="[+jot.link.current:esc+]"><img src="[(base_url)]manager/
includes/veriword.php?rand=[+jot.seed+]" width="148" height="60"
alt="If you have trouble reading the code, click on the code itself to
generate a new random code." style="border: 1px solid #003399" /></
a></div>
Security Code:<br /><input type="text" name="vericode"
                style="width:150px;" size="20" /> 
    `:strip+]

    <div style="float:right;width: 100px;"></div>
    <input tabindex="[+jot.seed:math=`?+5`+]" name="submit"
type="submit" value="[+form.edit:is=`1`:then=`Save Comment`:else=`Post
Comment`+]" />
    [+form.edit:is=`1`:then=`
        <input tabindex="[+jot.seed:math=`?+5`+]" name="submit"
type="submit" value="Cancel" onclick="history.go(-1);return false;" />
    `+]
    </fieldset>
</form>
```

Let us test what we have learned by just copying this code without any change to the comments chunk. And then preview it. You will see the same form that you saw before mentioning a custom chunk for it.

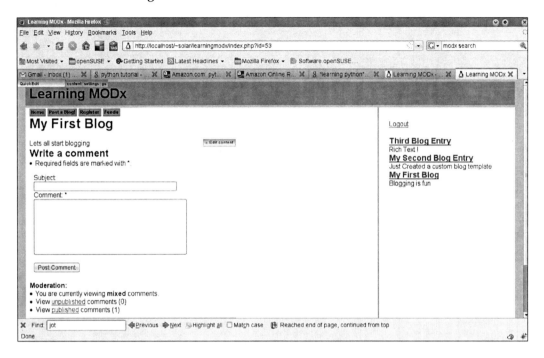

The above template uses PHx, which is explained in the next chapter. For now, let us just do a simple modification of the rendered form. Modify the chunk comments in line two from:

```
<h2>[+form.edit:is=`1`:then=`Edit comment`:else=`Write a
                                     comment`+]</h2>
```

to:

```
<b>[+form.edit:is=`1`:then=`Edit comment`:else=`Write a
                                     comment`+]</b>
```

Preview any comments page and it will look similar to the following:

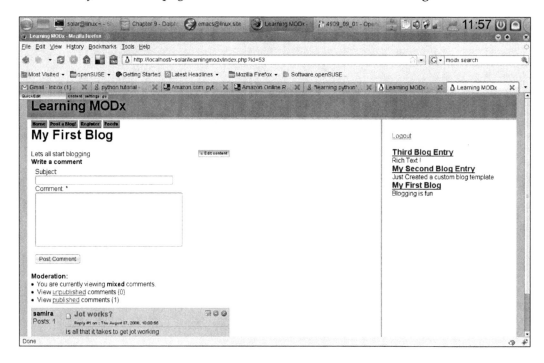

We have successfully changed the appearance of a specific element of the form from a heading to just bold text. Although we have just changed a line, using the same principles you have just learned, you can change the appearance of the form to make it look anyway you like.

Placeholders

Placeholders are similar to variables that can be placed within a chunk or a template. In the place of the placeholder, whatever value the snippet assigns to the placeholder will be inserted into the chunk or template during the processing of the snippet code. As we have already seen, most snippets provide placeholders that can be used in an HTML document, such as the `wayfinder` snippet, which we came across earlier in the previous chapter on lists.

Snippets like Jot provide many uses for placeholders. In the case of Jot, it has a comment form and the comments themselves. Maybe you want to change the order in which the details of comments are displayed by default. To do this, we can send appropriate parameters to tell Jot to not output anything, but rather to set values for the placeholders that contain the details for the individual elements. And then, we can place those placeholders in the templates in the order we want. As an example, right now the comments are shown below the comment form. Let us go ahead and change this behavior to show the comments form after the comments. The first step is to let Jot know that we are not expecting one whole output that gets inserted in the place where Jot was called, but rather we want the separate elements in the placeholders. To do that, change the call to Jot in the Learning MODx blog template to contain &placeholders=`1` & output=`0`.

```
[!Jot? &placeholders=`1` &output=`0` &tplForm=`comments`
                         &canpost=`Registered Users`!]
```

Now if you preview any post, you will notice that the comments and the comment form have disappeared. This is as good as not having made a call to Jot at all. However, there is one difference, which is that now we have placeholders that contain the output and we can place them anywhere in the template.

Few of the available Jot placeholders are:

- [+jot.html.navigation+] — places the navigation on the page
- [+jot.html.comments+] — places the comment on the page
- [+jot.html.moderate+] — places the moderation info on the page
- [+jot.html.form+] — places the form on the page

Let us use these placeholders in the Learning MODx blog template to get the form, comments, moderation info, and the navigation in the order that we want. Change the contents of the Learning MODx blog template to the following:

```
<!DOCTYPE html PUBLIC "-//W3C//DTD XHTML 1.1//EN" "http://www.w3.org/
TR/xhtml11/DTD/xhtml11.dtd"> <html xmlns="http://www.w3.org/1999/
xhtml" xml:lang="en">
 <head>
  <title>Learning MODx</title>
  <meta http-equiv="Content-Type" content="text/html; charset=iso-
                                               8859-1" />
  <link rel="stylesheet" type="text/css" href="style.css" />
 </head>
 <body>
  <div id="banner">
   <h1>Learning MODx</h1>
  </div>

  <div id="wrapper">
   <div id="container">
   <div id="content">
    <div id="col-1">

<div id="menu">
```

```
[!Wayfinder?startId=`0` &amp;level=`2` &amp;outerClass=`outer`
&amp;innerClass='inner' &amp;lastClass=`last` &amp;firstClass=`first`
&amp;hereClass=`active`!]
</div>
      <h1>[*pagetitle*]</h1>
      <br/>

      [*#content*]
<br>
[!Jot? &placeholders=1 &output=0 &tplForm=`comments`
                       &canpost=`Registered Users`!]

<hr/>
[+jot.html.comments+]
[+jot.html.form+]
<hr/>
[+jot.html.moderate+]

      </div>

      <div id="col-2" >
       <div > [!WebLogin!] </div>

        <div>
        [!Ditto? &parents=`47` &tpl=`dittofrontpage`!]
        </div>
      </div>

     </div>

     </div>
     <div class="clearing"> </div>
    </div> <!-- end of wrapper div -->
    <div id="footer">It is fun and exciting to build websites with
                                        MODx</div></body>
   </html>
```

Now, if you preview the page, you will notice the elements of the comment
functionality in the order we wanted. We also have the flexibility to insert any
HTML between the placeholders. In the preceding case, we have just inserted
a horizontal line.

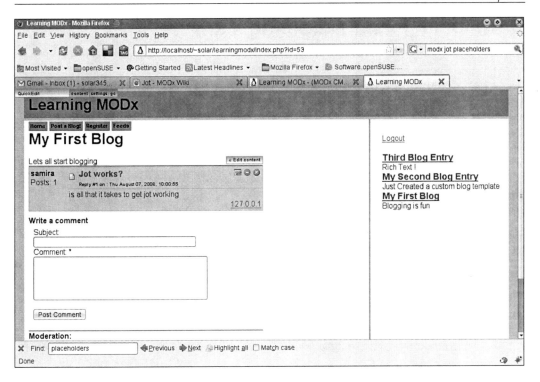

Using non-bundled snippets

Now that we have learned how to discover how to use the snippets that come bundled with MODx, let us explore how to use new snippets that are available online. For this example, we will consider one snippet called DittoCal. DittoCal allows navigation of the blog based on dates.

Installing a snippet

To install a snippet, you have to perform one or more of the following three steps:

1. Download and extract the snippet.
2. Create a snippet using the MODx Manager interface with the available snippet code.
3. Copy the required files to the appropriate directory.

Downloading and extracting a snippet

MODx snippets can be downloaded from `http://www.MODxcms.com/resources.html`. The DittoCal snippet can be downloaded from `http://MODxcms.com/DittoCal-696.html`. Once downloaded, you will have a ZIP file. Extract it the same way as you extracted MODx in the first chapter. Notice that, though the procedure for installing most custom snippets is the same as what is being explained here, it always helps to read the installation instructions that are available in the snippet download page, or in a ReadMe, file after extracting the snippet.

Adding a snippet

Now that you have downloaded and extracted a snippet, to be able to use it, you have to create a snippet using the MODx Manager interface. To do this, follow these steps:

1. Click on the **Manage Resources** menu item from the **Resources** menu.
2. Click on the **Snippets** tab.
3. Click on **New Snippet**.
4. Fill in the appropriate details using the code from the extracted snippet files. For our example, it will be:

Field Name	Value
Snippet Name	DittoCal
Description	Access Posts based on dates
Snippet code	From the extracted file snippet.DittoCal.php

Note that the description is for your reference only. When you click on the snippets tab, the description you see of the snippets is taken from this field. The name that you give here is exactly what you will be using in the code when you want to call the snippet. All snippets that you download will have a file that looks similar to `snippet.snippetname.php`, which is a file that will contain the code to be used as the snippet code. Remember the content area for snippet code requires the actual code from that snippet file copied and pasted, and not the name of the snippet file. When you copy-paste from the snippet code, make sure you don't get duplicate `<?php...?>` tags in the source. You can get by without the PHP tags; the Manager will automatically insert a set, if necessary, when saving the snippet to the database.

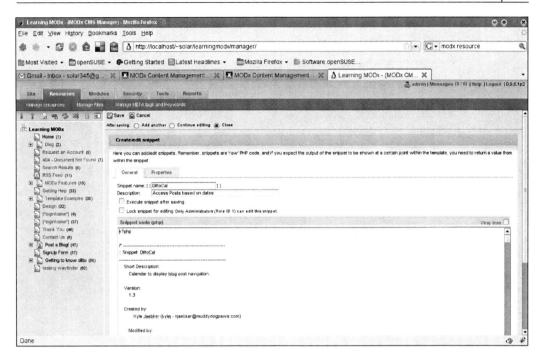

The image above shows the page for adding a snippet. In this page, you can give the snippet details such as the name, description, and the snippet code itself.

Copying required files

Some snippets that you download will have files that are required for the snippet to work and need to be placed in the appropriate directory. In most cases, these files will have to be placed in a specific folder within a directory assets/snippets, within the MODx root directory. Generally, you will have to create a folder with the snippet name inside the assests/snippets folder and place all the required files there. Most snippets come with the complete folder structure when you extract them, which includes assets/snippets/snippetname. In such a case, you can copy the folder directly to the MODx root directory. Some snippets also have installers that do this for you. For our example snippet, we will do it as is mentioned in the DittoCal snippet instructions.

1. Create a folder called DittoCal in the assets/snippets directory.

2. Copy the file `JSON.php` from the extracted folder to `assets/snippets/DittoCal`.

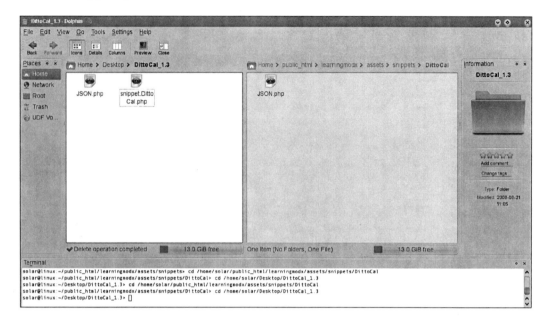

Using the snippet

The previous sections of this chapter explained how to do research on any snippet that you may come across. For our example, we are looking at the DittoCal snippet. The usage of DittoCal is slightly different from the other snippets that we have used so far. The way to use a snippet is generally documented in the file from which you get the code for the snippet that you create. For our example, this is an excerpt from the JSON.php file.

```
Required Usage:
   [!DittoCal?calSource=``!]

   You must create a new document with the following settings:
     template: blank
     show in menu: no
     published: yes
     searchable: no
     content type: text/plain
     document content:
     [!Ditto? &parents=`yourblogfolder` &display=`all`
                                       &format=`json`!]

   This document is used to output your post data so that it
```

```
can be read into the calendar. You should set the startId
to your blog folder and set summarize to the max number
of posts you expect to have. Leave everything else the same
as above.
```

As you can see from the preceding text, this snippet, besides having to be called from a template or a document, also needs a new document to be created with a call to another snippet. We have chosen this snippet to demonstrate that each snippet has its own way of functioning, and the only way you can get to know how to use them for the functionality you require is by reading through any documentation that is available on the snippet. In this case, it was the comments in the source code itself. Generally, all snippets will have such usage comments at the top of the code, so that it is easy for those who use it to get to it. Some snippets come with well-formatted documentation that may be in the extracted folder as an html file or txt file, or a set of them within a docs folder. Remember, these are snippets that are created by individual users, and everyone documents their snippet in their own way. Now, let us go ahead and use the snippet in our site.

Create a document with the following details:

Field Name	Field Value
Title	DittoCal
Content	[!Ditto? &parents=`47` &display=`all` &format=`json`!] (Replace 47 with whatever is the ID of the Post a Blog! document)
Template	Blank
Content Type	Text/Plain
Shown in Menu	No

Edit the code of the Learning MODx default template to include the call to Dittocal:

```
<!DOCTYPE html PUBLIC "-//W3C//DTD XHTML 1.1//EN" "http://www.w3.org/
TR/xhtml11/DTD/xhtml11.dtd"> <html xmlns="http://www.w3.org/1999/
xhtml" xml:lang="en">
 <head>
  <title>Learning MODx</title>
  <meta http-equiv="Content-Type" content="text/html; charset=iso-
                                                          8859-1" />
  <link rel="stylesheet" type="text/css" href="style.css" />
 </head>
 <body>
  <div id="banner">
   <h1>Learning MODx</h1>
  </div>
```

```
    <div id="wrapper">
     <div id="container">
     <div id="content">
      <div id="col-1">
<div id="menu">
[!Wayfinder?startId=`0` &amp;level=`2` &amp;outerClass=`outer`
&amp;innerClass='inner' &amp;lastClass=`last` &amp;firstClass=`first`
&amp;hereClass=`active`!]
</div>
        <h1>[*pagetitle*]</h1>
        <br/>

        [*#content*]
      </div>

        <div id="col-2" >

        <div > [!WebLogin!] </div>

          <div>
          [!Ditto? &parents=`47` &tpl=`dittofrontpage`!]
          </div>
<div>
[!DittoCal?calSource=`64` !]
</div>
      </div>

      </div>

    </div>
     <div class="clearing"> </div>
    </div> <!-- end of wrapper div -->
    <div id="footer">It is fun and exciting to build websites with
                                        MODx</div></body>
  </html>
```

Notice that the value of the calSource parameter must be the ID of the document that you just created. Replace 64 with the ID of your DittoCal document.

Snippet without dependent files

Some snippets don't require any files. For such snippets, we don't have to do step 3. An example of such a snippet is tagcloud.

Snippeting skills

Finding the right snippet for the right functionality is a skill in itself. There are many ways to search for the right snippet. First, you need to identify apt specific words that explain what you want your snippet to do, and then you can use a search engine with those words and 'MODx'. You should also search in the MODx forums, as mentioned in chapter 2. Finally, you can browse through the MODx resource page. The tag cloud in the resource page makes it easy to locate snippets based on categories. If you are not able to find what you are looking for, you can also ask in the forums.

Summary

In this chapter, we have learned how to use the hundreds of snippets available in detail. We have also learned how to search for snippets that do not come packaged with MODx and how to use them. Along the way, we have added the functionality to post comments and to navigate posts through date.

9
PHx

We have learned how to develop our MODx site by using templates, documents, and chunks, along with snippets. Snippets provide the power of having decisions made and interacting with the databases. Or, in short, the logical component is abstracted to the snippets, whereas the documents, templates, and chunks provide a way to show the contents returned by a snippet or the contents of a variable. In some cases, it may be necessary to perform simple conditional checks in the documents, or templates themselves. **PHx — Place Holders extended —** is a set of notations that makes this possible by adding a logic layer directly to the placeholder. PHx also makes it possible to format the output, for example converting the string to uppercase, and so on. In this chapter, we will learn to use this notation.

PHx in action

Let us learn our need of PHx by building a new functionality for our site that lets us add profiles of our family members and friends. We will add a new page called 'Family and Friends' that will show the list of all the individuals that we add. Once the user clicks on an individual, it will show certain details such as name, relationship to you, occupation, web site. This is easy to implement; all we have to do is create the template variables for each of the fields, and create a template that uses these template variables. So, to display the Occupation, the template will have a code similar to the following:

```
Occupation: [*occupation*]
```

Though this might appear to work initially, it has a small glitch in it. When we are entering the personal details of an individual, we may not want to enter all of the values for every individual. In the case of not having a value for the variable, it looks cleaner to not show the label at all instead of leaving it blank. In our case — if we have no value for occupation — it will look cleaner to not show the label **Occupation**. So here comes a need for displaying certain text only if the template variable — in this case, occupation — has a value. We can do this using PHx without having to write a snippet.

Field Name	Field Value
Variable Name	website
Input Type	URL
Template Access	Family and Friends
Existing Category	Learning MODx

5. Now that we have the template variables, let us create the template that the documents representing members will use. Create a template with the following details. The highlighted section of the code represents the portion that introduces the situation discussed in the beginning of the chapter. Even if the template variable has no value, there is a corresponding label shown, because we have it so in the template.

Field Name	Field Value
Template name	Family and Friends
Existing Category	Learning MODx
Template Code	Code given next

Template Code:

```
<!DOCTYPE html PUBLIC "-//W3C//DTD XHTML 1.1//EN" "http://www.w3.org/
TR/xhtml11/DTD/xhtml11.dtd"> <html xmlns="http://www.w3.org/1999/
xhtml" xml:lang="en">
  <head>
    <title>Learning MODx</title>
    <meta http-equiv="Content-Type" content="text/html; charset=iso-
                                              8859-1" />
    <link rel="stylesheet" type="text/css" href="style.css" />
  </head>
  <body>
    <div id="banner">
      <h1>Learning MODx</h1>
    </div>

    <div id="wrapper">
      <div id="container">
        <div id="content">
          <div id="col-1">
<div id="menu">
[!Wayfinder?startId=`0` &amp;level=`2` &amp;outerClass=`outer`
&amp;innerClass='inner' &amp;lastClass=`last` &amp;firstClass=`first`
&amp;hereClass=`active`!]
</div>
```

```
            <h1>[*pagetitle*]</h1>
            <br/>
<table>
<tr> <td> Relationship: </td> <td> [*relationship*] </td> </tr>
<tr> <td> Occupation: </td> <td>  [*occupation*] </td> </tr>
<tr> <td> Website: </td> <td>  [*website*] </td> </tr>
</table>
<br/>

[*#content*]

     </div>

     <div id="col-2" >

       <div > [!WebLogin!] </div>

             <div>
                [!Ditto? &parents=`47` &tpl=`dittofrontpage`!]
             </div>

        </div>

     </div>

        </div>
     <div class="clearing"> </div>
  </div> <!-- end of wrapper div -->
  <div id="footer">It is fun and exciting to build websites with
                                   MODx</div></body>

</html>
```

Now that we have the template for Family and Friends, let us create a few documents that represent members. We will use these documents to observe the transformations in the appearance as we proceed.

Field Name	Field Value
Title	Richard Stallman
Uses Template	Family and Friends
Show in menu	Unchecked
Document parent	Family and Friends
Document content	Richard Stallman is the founder of , FSF, and GNU Emacs!
relationship	Friend
occupation	Geek
website	http://www.stallman.org

Field Name	Field Value
Title	Richard Bandler
Uses Template	Family and Friends
Show in menu	Unchecked
Document parent	Family and Friends
Document content	Founder of Neuro Linguistic Programming (NLP)
relationship	Friend
occupation	
website	http://www.richardbandler.com

Preview the **Family and Friends** document and you should see the following image:

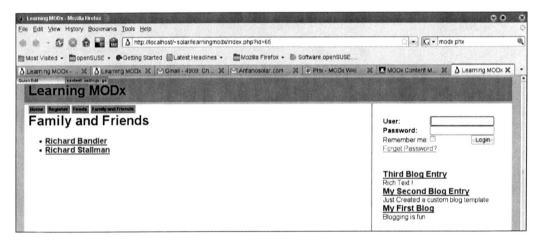

Now preview the test documents and you should see the following screens:

Notice that the **Occupation** field in the last screenshot has been left blank. This does not look clean. We will go ahead and fix this by amending the Family and Friends template to include the highlighted segment of code:

```
<!DOCTYPE html PUBLIC "-//W3C//DTD XHTML 1.1//EN" "http://www.w3.org/
TR/xhtml11/DTD/xhtml11.dtd"> <html xmlns="http://www.w3.org/1999/
xhtml" xml:lang="en">
  <head>
    <title>Learning MODx</title>
    <meta http-equiv="Content-Type" content="text/html; charset=iso-
                                                              8859-1" />
    <link rel="stylesheet" type="text/css" href="style.css" />
  </head>
  <body>
    <div id="banner">
      <h1>Learning MODx</h1>
    </div>

    <div id="wrapper">
      <div id="container">
        <div id="content">
          <div id="col-1">
<div id="menu">
[!Wayfinder?startId=`0` &amp;level=`2` &amp;outerClass=`outer`
&amp;innerClass='inner' &amp;lastClass=`last` &amp;firstClass=`first`
&amp;hereClass=`active`!]
</div>

        <h1>[*pagetitle*]</h1>
        <br/>
<table>

<tr> <td> Relationship: </td> <td> [*relationship*] </td> </tr>

[+phx:if=`[*occupation*]`:is=``:then=``:else=`<tr> <td> Occupation:
                    </td> <td>  [*occupation*] </td> </tr>`+]

<tr> <td> Website: </td> <td>  [*website*] </td> </tr>

</table>
<br/>

[*#content*]

          </div>

      <div id="col-2" >

        <div > [!WebLogin!]   </div>
            <div>
              [!Ditto? &parents=`47` &tpl=`dittofrontpage`!]
```

```
                </div>
        </div>
            </div>
        </div>
        <div class="clearing"> </div>
    </div> <!-- end of wrapper div -->
    <div id="footer">It is fun and exciting to build websites with
                                                    MODx</div>
</body>
</html>
```

Now preview the second test document again:

Notice that the label **Occupation** has disappeared. We still have to make sure that it is appearing in the first test document, as the first test document does have a value in the `occupation` field.

The preview of the first test document is as follows:

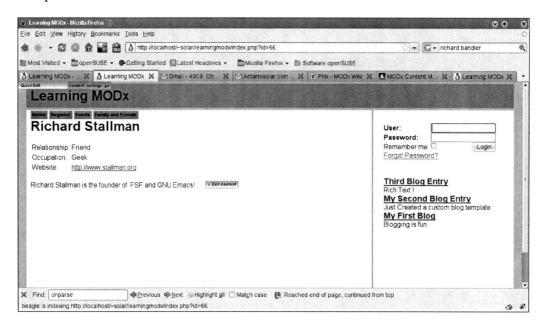

Now that we have learned how to hide the labels when the corresponding template variables are empty, we can continue to do the same for the rest of the template variables. Modify the template code to look like the following:

```
<!DOCTYPE html PUBLIC "-//W3C//DTD XHTML 1.1//EN" "http://www.w3.org/
TR/xhtml11/DTD/xhtml11.dtd"> <html xmlns="http://www.w3.org/1999/
xhtml" xml:lang="en">
  <head>
    <title>Learning MODx</title>
    <meta http-equiv="Content-Type" content="text/html; charset=iso-
                                                      8859-1" />
    <link rel="stylesheet" type="text/css" href="style.css" />
  </head>
  <body>
    <div id="banner">

      <h1>Learning MODx</h1>

    </div>

    <div id="wrapper">
      <div id="container">
        <div id="content">
          <div id="col-1">
    <div id="menu">
```

```
[!Wayfinder?startId=`0` &amp;level=`2` &amp;outerClass=`outer`
&amp;innerClass='inner' &amp;lastClass=`last` &amp;firstClass=`first`
&amp;hereClass=`active`!]
</div>
        <h1>[*pagetitle*]</h1>
        <br/>
<table>
[+phx:if=`[*relationship*]`:is=``:then=``:else=`<tr> <td>
 Relationship: </td> <td> [*relationship*] </td> </tr>`+]
[+phx:if=`[*occupation*]`:is=``:then=``:else=`<tr> <td> Occupation:
                   </td> <td>   [*occupation*] </td> </tr>`+]
[+phx:if=`[*website*]`:is=``:then=``:else=`<tr> <td> Website: </td>
                   <td>   [*website*] </td> </tr>`+]

</table>
<br/>

[*#content*]

          </div>

     <div id="col-2" >

        <div > [!WebLogin!]   </div>

              <div>
                 [!Ditto? &parents=`47` &tpl=`dittofrontpage`!]
              </div>

     </div>


         </div>
       </div>
      <div class="clearing"> </div>
   </div> <!-- end of wrapper div -->
   <div id="footer">It is fun and exciting to build websites with
                                   MODx</div></body>

</html>
```

Now take a moment to analyze the format of the highlighted code. The notation is quite intuitive. The next section explains this notation in detail.

The PHx notation

Now that we have discovered in what situations PHx becomes helpful, we will now learn more about the syntax of PHx.

Simple usage

PHx allows any template variable to be formatted using a simple format. The format is generally like this: `[+templatevariablename:modifier+]`. You can use the `[+ +]` syntax, or the `[* *]`, syntax just like you do for any other template variable.

Modifiers are special keywords that transform the value of the template variable. We have modifiers to turn the string to uppercase, lowercase, the first character to uppercase, and so on.

For example: If we have a template variable `Occupation` with the value `business`, then `[+occupation:ucfirst+]` will return `Business`.

The following is a list of the most commonly used modifiers:

- `lcase` — returns the current value with all the alphabetic characters converted to lowercase. For example:
  - If `[+occupation+]` outputs `Engineer`, `[+occupation:lcase+]` will output `engineer`

- `ucase` — returns the current value with all the alphabetic characters converted to uppercase. For example:
  - If `[+occupation+]` outputs `Engineer`, `[+occupation:ucase+]` will output `ENGINEER`

- `ucfirst` — returns the current value's first character as uppercase. For example:
  - If `[+occupation+]` outputs `engineer`, `[+occupation: ucfirst+]` will output `Engineer`

- `len` — returns the length of the current value. For example:
  - If `[+occupation+]` outputs `engineer`, `[+occupation:len+]` will output `8`.

- `select=`options`` — options like `value1=output1&value2=output2`

Notice that the last modifier accepts a value after the = sign. The `select` modifier accepts values of the format described after the = sign. For example, if you would like to output one for 1, two for 2, three for 3, and the template variable has the values 1, or 2, or 3, you will do this by using the `select` modifier as shown next:

```
[+templatevariablename:select=`1=one&2=two&3=three`+]
```

For a complete list of the modifiers, you can refer to the MODx wiki (`http://wiki.MODxcms.com/index.php/PHx`).

Conditional statements

Besides the preceding listed modifiers that format the given template variable, we can also have conditional statements that perform an action based on a decision made. The general structure of a conditional statement is as follows:

```
[+templatevariablename:condition:then=`template`:else=`template`+]
```

Here, `template` can be simple HTML or a chunk name, or even a snippet.

Conditions are of the form:

```
conditional operator = `value`
```

An example of a condition is:

```
:is=`1`
```

An example of a conditional statement is:

```
[+flag:is=`1`:then=`onchunk`:else=`offchunk`+]
```

The following is a list of the different conditional operators and their meanings:

- `is` — is equal to.
- `ne` — is not equal to.
- `eg` — is equal or greater than.
- `el` — is equal or lower than.
- `gt` — is greater than.
- `lt` — is lower than.
- `mo=`Webgroups`` — is the current logged in user a member of any of the given list of webgroups? The list of webgroups is separated by commas.

With these conditions, you can check if a template variable is equal to or greater than some value, and then display a chunk if it is or another one if it is not.

Usage with the PHx placeholder

For some expression, we might want to make use of a dummy placeholder instead of a template variable. In such cases, we can use the PHx placeholder. We will look into such examples next.

Let us say we are using PHx to display the username of the current logged in user. To do this, we will use the `userinfo` modifier. We have already learned that modifiers are used on template variables or placeholders. In the case of this modifier, we don't have to explicitly mention the placeholder, as `userinfo` can act only on the placeholder that stores the user's ID. In such situations, we will use the dummy placeholder phx:

For example:

```
[+phx:userinfo=`username`+]
```

Another example is the mo operation. mo allows us to check if the current logged in user is a member of any of the given webgroups. Again, here we are acting based on the logged in user's ID. Hence we will need to use the dummy placeholder PHx.

For example:

```
[+phx:mo=`friends`: then=`You belong to the friends group`:else=`You
                        do not belong to the friends group`+]
```

There are two other situations where you will be using the PHx placeholder:

- **Multiple Conditions**: This is when you want to make a decision based on one or more conditions. Multiple conditions are explained in the next subsection.

- When using the required placeholder in more than one place in the expression:
  ```
  [+phx:if=`[*occupation*]`:is=``:then=``:else=`<tr> <td>
     Occupation: </td> <td>  [*occupation*] </td> </tr>`+]
  ```

Notice that the template variable `[*occupation*]` is used in the condition and in the output. Use of the `if` keyword is explained in the next subsection.

Multiple conditions

To be able to use multiple conditions, you must first know how to use the `if` keyword. We have learned how to check the template variable for a given condition. But how do we do the same when we use the dummy placeholder `phx`? We need to have a format to specify which template variable we are evaluating to test the given condition. We can do this with the following syntax.

```
:if=`*templatevariable*`
```

After the `if` keyword followed by the template variable, the syntax remains the same. You still have to write a condition and specify what to show if the condition is true and what to show if the condition is not. When using this syntax, multiple conditions are easy. All you need to do is use `:and` or `:or` and specify a new condition. When using `:or`, the entire expression is true if any one of the conditions is true. When using `:and`, the entire expression is true only if all the conditions are true.

Summary

In this chapter, we have learned how to format the values in template variables, and have also seen how to make conditions based on the values of template variables and accordingly present a different output either from the HTML in the expression or from a chunk or snippet. We have also, in the process of learning PHx, added a *Family and Friends* feature to the site, which allows us to create and display the profiles of the individuals. We have demonstrated how the usage of PHx can help us hide labels when the corresponding values are empty.

10
Simple Recipes

We have learned the core concepts that are necessary to build a site using MODx. In this chapter, we will use what we have already learned, to study how certain commonly required functionalities can be implemented. We will learn how to integrate a forum, image gallery, forms that can send mail, create web user profiles, and identify similar posts for blogs.

Forums

Forums are discussion boards that allow a user to post the information on a topic. Following a post, users can reply to the post, and hence create a threaded discussion. Forums are generally used for discussions. In a MODx site, one simple method to implement a forum is using the **SMF** module. SMF is an open source community forum software application that can be installed independently of MODx. The SMF module for MODx allows the integration of MODx with SMF. This allows a user to log in once in the MODx site and use the SMF forum as well, which means your site can be powered by MODx, and can take advantage of the forum-specific functionalities of third-party software. We will see how the SMF modules make it possible. The following are the steps to get SMF working with MODx.

1. Install SMF.
2. Install the SMF module for MODx.

Installing SMF

As mentioned earlier, SMF is fourm-specific software that we are going to use with MODx. So we will have to download and install SMF independently.

1. Download SMF from `http://download.simplemachines.org/index.php?thanks;filename=smf_1-1-5_install.zip`.
2. Extract the contents of the archive inside a folder called `forum`.

3. Copy the `forum` folder to the root of the MODx installation.

4. Visit the MODx site that we have been developing by suffixing `/forum` at the end; for example, `http://localhost/~solar/learningMODx/forum`.

   If you see something like the following screen, then you must change the permissions on the folders and their contents to let the web server have read and write permissions. More information on permission issues has been given in Chapter 2.

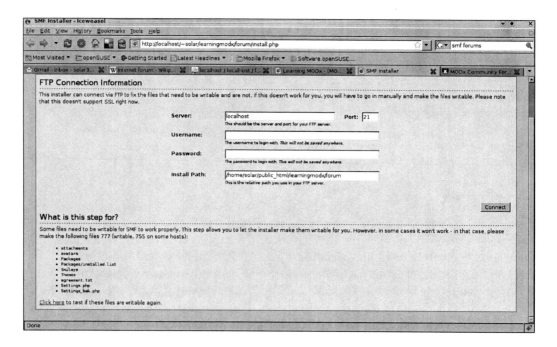

5. You will see something like the following.

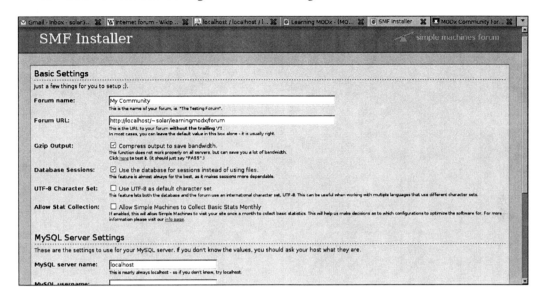

Change the following details:

Field Name	Field Value
Forum Name	Learning MODx Forum.
Forum URL	The MODx site path suffixed with a /forum;
	for example, http://localhost/~solar/learningMODx/forum.
MySQL username	Whatever you gave for the MODx installation (Chapter 1).
MySQL password	Whatever you gave for the MODx installation (Chapter 1).

If the given MYSQL username and password do not have permissions to create a new database, then you will have to create the database mentioned yourself (Refer to Chapter 1).

You should now see a screen like the following:

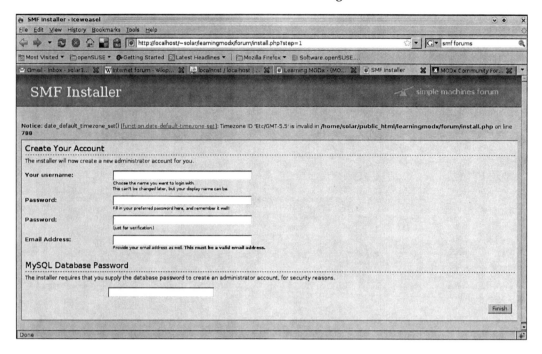

6. Fill in the following details and click **Next**.

Field Name	Field Value
Your username	Any username that you will use to administer the forum. For this example, leave it as admin.
Password	Password for the above user. For this example, give the same password you gave for MODx admin user.
MySQL Database Password	The MySQL password that you gave in the previous screen.

If everything went fine, you should see a page like the following:

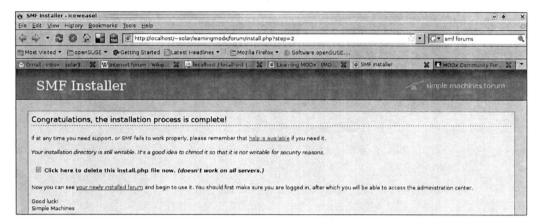

7. Click on the newly installed forum link to see what the forum looks like:

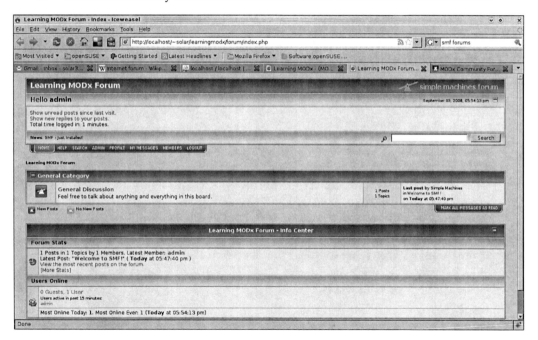

Installing the SMF module

Now that we have a working installation of SMF, we need to install the SMF module for MODx, to integrate MODx with SMF.

1. Download the SMF module from the MODx repository (http://MODxcms. com/SMF-Forum-Integration-918.html).

2. Extract the downloaded folder.

3. Copy the `install` folder to the MODx root directory.

4. Copy the contents of the `asset` folder to the `asset` folder in the MODx root directory.

5. Open the MODx URL with a `/install` suffix (for example: http://localhost/~solar/learningMODx/install/).

6. Click **Next** on the screen you see after opening the above URL.

7. With the checkbox selected for the module and the plug-in, click **Install Now**.

8. **After installation** click **Close** and it will redirect you to the MODx Manager page.

9. Click on the **Manage Modules** menu item in the **Modules** menu.

10. Click on **SMF Connector**, and click on the **Configuration** tab.

11. Fill in the following values:

Field Name	Field Value
CMS base URL	The base URL of the site after the domain name — for example: `/~solar/learningMODx/`
Forum base path	The full path of the SMF installation — for example: `/home/ solar/public_html/learningMODx/forum`
Admin User	The admin user name for the forum — in our example, *admin*
Admin password	The admin password for the forum that you had created when installing SMF
Login page	1
Logout page	1

12. Click on the **Save** button.

13. Click on the **SMF Connector** menu item in the **Modules** menu.

14. Click on **Synchronize Users**, and click **OK** when asked if you really want to synchronize.

"Synchronize Users" means that the users that you have added in MODx are also created as users in SMF. Now that you have synchronized user accounts, you can test them. Log out of the MODx, and log in as the user that we created earlier: *samira*. Now open the forum URL, which is in our installation of the MODx site URL suffixed with `/forum` (for example, `http://localhost/~solar/learningMODx/forum`). The screen should look like the following.

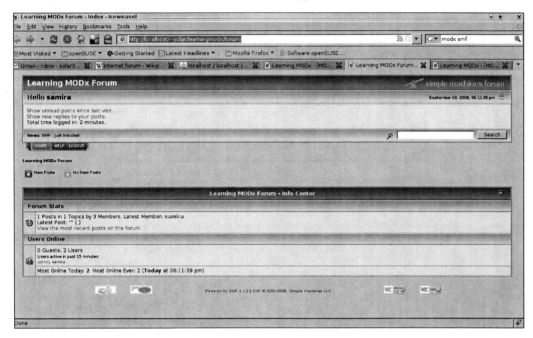

Notice that it says **Hello samira**, and the user didn't have to log in again. Hence we have successfully integrated MODx with a forum application.

Note that it may be necessary to give SMF the same look and feel as the rest of your site, for which you will have to theme SMF. We will not discuss theming SMF in this book.

Image gallery

MODx has many sophisticated image gallery snippets that allow you to create an image gallery anywhere in the site. For this example, we will be using the `MaxiGallery` snippet. To get the image gallery working, install the snippet as explained in the chapter on snippets.

1. Download the snippet from the MODx repository `http://MODxcms.com/MaxiGallery-532.html`.

2. Extract the snippet.

3. Create a new snippet with the name `MaxiGallery`, and place the contents of `maxigallery.txt` as the snippet code.

4. Copy the `assets` directory within the extracted folder to the root of the installation. Note that it contains two folders that are to be copied:

   ○ `assets/galleries` (Make sure that `assets/galleries` has write permissions)

   ○ `assets/snippets/maxigallery`

5. To test the snippet, create a document with the following details:

Field Name	Field Value
Title	Gallery
Uses template	Learning MODx default template
Document content	`[!MaxiGallery!]`

6. Preview the page and you will see something like the following; note the **Manage pictures** button where the snippet code was placed:

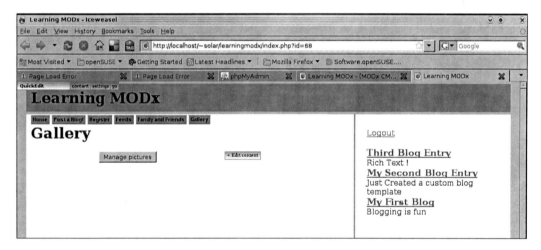

7. When you click on **Manage Pictures**, you will see something like the following:

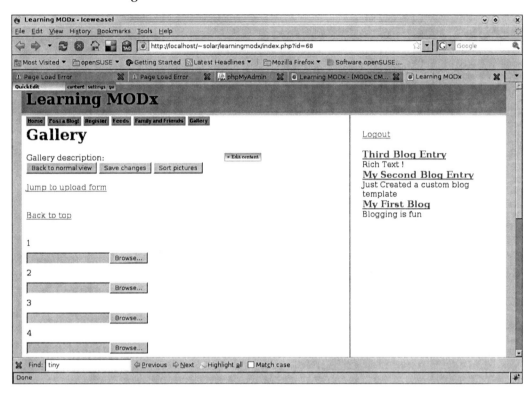

8. Select a couple of photos using the **Browse...** button and click **Upload**. Then **Save changes** and click on **Back to normal view**. You will see something like the following:

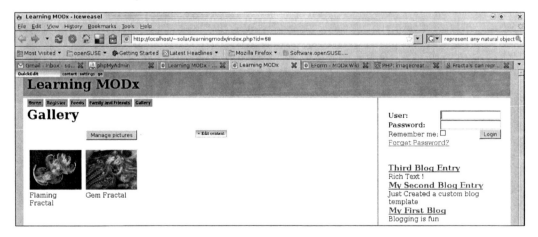

9. When you click on any of the photos, you will see something like the following:

Note that the **Manage pictures** button appears only when you have logged in as an admin in the Manager, or if the web user group that the current logged in user belongs to has edit permissions on the document. We have successfully created an image gallery. But that's not all; MaxiGallery gives us even more flexibility. For example, you can try the following snippet as the document content:

```
[!MaxiGallery? &display=`embedded` &embedtype=`slimbox` !]
```

Now notice how the screen looks when you click on any of the pictures:

As you can see, the way the gallery is presented now is much better than just placing images in a document. Similarly, you can add many more effects and completely customize the way `MaxiGallery` displays the gallery using its parameters and placeholders. For more information on learning how to customize a snippet, read the chapter on snippets. What we have shown here is just the beginning; you can combine multiple snippets to come up with interesting ideas and solutions. A popular example is using MaxiGallery and jot for photo blogging. Going through each scenario and presenting the solution would be beyond the scope of this book, but this chapter intends to get you started with learning to find creative solutions yourself.

Emailing from forms

In this section, we will discuss how to create HTML forms in MODx that can send mail to the moderator of the site. Such forms are often used as enquiry forms or feedback forms. When a user inputs some information, the moderator gets a mail with the details. In MODx, you can achieve this by using the `eForm` snippet. `eForm` can also validate the form before sending out the mail. The `eForm` snippet comes bundled with MODx and hence, you don't have to install it.

To start using `eForm`, let us create a document with the following details.

Field Name	Field Value
Title	Enquiry Form
Uses template	Learning MODx default template
Document content	[!eForm? &formid=`EnquiryForm` &subject=`[+subject+]` &to=`youremailid` &tpl=`EnquiryForm` &gotoid=`1` !]

Now, create a chunk with the name `EnquiryForm` and the content as given next:

```
<p class="error">[+validationmessage+]</p>

<form id="EnquireryForm"
method="post" action="[~[*id*]~]" >

    <fieldset>
        <h3> Enquiry Form</h3>

                Your name:
        <p><input name="name" id="Name" class="text" type="text"
                        eform="Your Name::1:" /></p></label>

        Your Email Address:
        <p><input name="email" id="Email" class="text" type="text"
                eform="Email Address:email:1" /></p> </label>

        Subject:
        <p><input name="subject" id="Subject" class="text" type="text"
                                eform="Subject::1" /></p> </label>

        Enquiry:
        <p><textarea name="enquiry" id="enquiry" eform=
                "Enquiry:textarea:1"></textarea></p>
        </label>

        <p><input type="submit" class="button" value="Enquire Now"
                                                /></p>

    </fieldset>
</form>
```

Now preview the document and you will see something like the following:

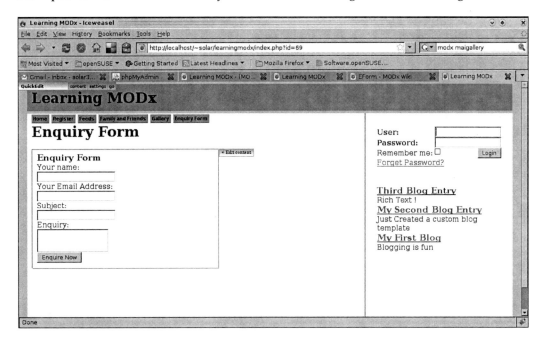

If you fill in the form and click on **Enquire Now**, it sends the user to the Home Page, and a mail is sent to the ID that you have given in the snippet call. If you see a page like the following, it means that MODx is not configured to use your mailing system. Refer to Chapter 1 to fix this.

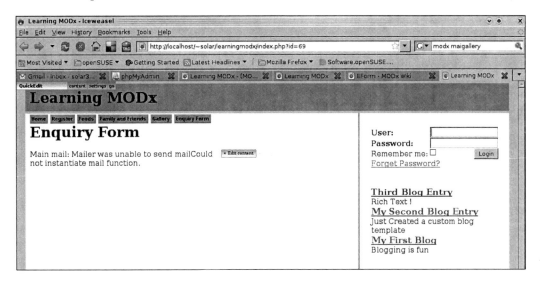

You must also note that the form comes with validation. Try submitting the empty form and you will see something like the following:

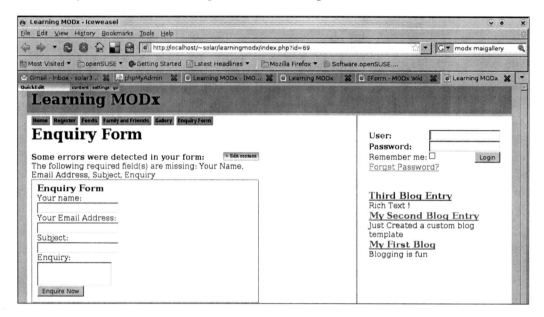

To understand what is happening, let us study the eForm snippet call:

```
[!eForm? &formid=`EnquiryForm` &subject=`[+subject+]` &to=
        `youremailid` &tpl=`EnquiryForm` &gotoid=`1` !]
```

We are making a call to eForm with various parameters, each of which is explained below.

- &to — the person to whom the mail has to be sent. If this parameter is omitted, the default "emailsender", as specified in the site configuration, will be used.

- &gotoid — which page has to be shown after sending the mail.

- &subject — what field in the form has to be used as the subject for the mail.

- &tpl — which chunk will be used as the form.

- &formid — it is possible to have multiple eForms in a same page. So, each form tag should have an id attribute.

Now let us have a look at the chunk code one piece at a time.

```
<form id="EnquireryForm"
method="post" action="[~[*id*]~]" >
```

The `id` attribute in the form tag is necessary to identify the form as related to the previous eForm snippet call. As mentioned in the explanation for the `&formid` parameter, this attribute takes a value that must be the same as the one given to the `&formid` parameter.

```
<p><input name="name" id="Name" class="text" type="text" eform="Your
                                                    Name::1:" /></p></label>
```

eForm forms are like any regular HTML forms; the only difference is that every field can use the `eform` attribute for validation. The `eform` attribute takes the values in the following format:

```
eform="[description/title]:[datatype]:[required]:[validation
                                    message]:[validation rule]"
```

The `description/title` you mention here is what will be shown during any validation message for that field. Note that all the elements shown above are optional and are separated by `:`. For the `input name` field above we have given `eform` the value `Your Name::1:`. The interpretation of this according to the format described above separated by `:` means that `Name` is the `description/title`, there is no specified datatype, `1` after the second colon denotes that it is a required or compulsory field, and there is no custom validation message nor any custom validation rule. There are different kinds of `datatype` allowing easy validation of the commonly used data types. The available list is:

- `string`—no specific validation besides checking if it's empty, and if the field is required
- `date`—checks if it is a valid date
- `integer`—checks if it is an integer
- `float`—checks if it is a number
- `email`—checks if it's a valid email address
- `file`—checks if a size error occurs, but does not check file type currently
- `html`—same as `string` except that it converts the line endings (`\n`) to `<br />` tags

The `required` option tells `eform` whether the field is a required field or not. For the `name` field, you can see that we have mentioned one indicating that it is a required field. `validation message` can be any message that you want to show when the field is empty and required, or is not of the given data type or doesn't fit into the validation rules. Finally, besides the given data types, you can also write custom validation rules. You can find more information on e-forms in the MODx wiki `http://wiki.MODxcms.com/index.php/EForm`.

User profiles

MODx allows us to implement user profiles using the `WebLoginPE` snippet. In this section, we will be using the `WebLoginPE` snippet to list the users, view their profile, and edit one's profile.

Installing WebLoginPE

`WebLoginPE` has a nice support site. You may want to look at `http://demo.scottydelicious.com/assets/snippets/webloginpe/docs/`.

1. Download the snippet from the MODx repository `http://MODxcms.com/WebLoginPE-1593.html`.

2. Extract the snippet.

3. Create a folder named `webloginpe` in the `assets/snippets` folder, in the root directory of the MODx installation.

4. Copy all the files of the extracted folder to the folder `assets/snippets/webloginpe`.

5. Create a new snippet using the MODx Manager with the name `WebLoginPE`, using the code from `webloginpe.snippet.php` from the extracted folder as the snippet code.

Edit profile

Now that we have `WebLoginPE` installed, let us use it.

```
[!WebLoginPE? &type=`profile`!]
```

A call to the snippet with the parameters and value as shown above lists all the users and allows the currently logged user to edit his/her profile. So let us create a document with the following details:

Field Name	Field Value
Title	My Profile
Uses template	Learning MODx default template
Show in menu	Unchecked
Document Content	`[!WebLoginPE? &type=`profile`!]`

Now, log in as *samira* in the site, and preview this page. You will see something like the following:

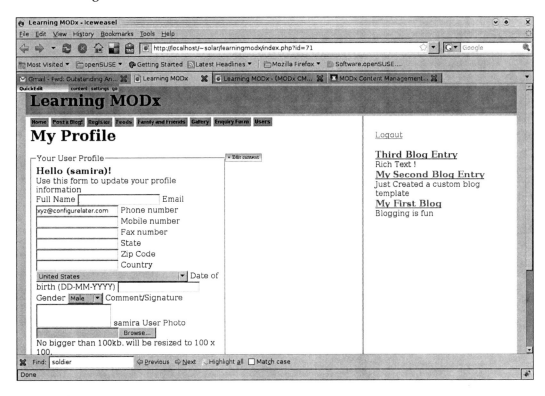

You can change some value and notice that the changes get saved and the new values are shown when you edit the profile again. The default profile edit for the user has many common fields such as the full name, email ID, photo, and so on. You can also change the fields and the look of the edit form using chunks. We leave that as an exercise for the reader.

List users and view profile

To list the users and view their profile, create a document with the following details:

Field Name	Field Value
Title	Users
Uses template	Learning MODx default template
Document Content	[!WebLoginPE? &type=`users`!]

Now if you preview this page, it will look like the following, which lists all the users of the site:

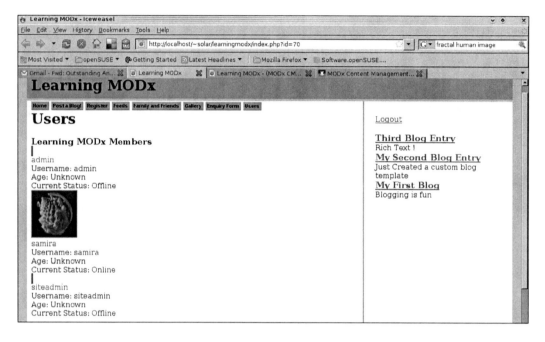

If you click on any user, it will show that user's profile as in the following image. The Profile View page also has provision for sending a message to the user.

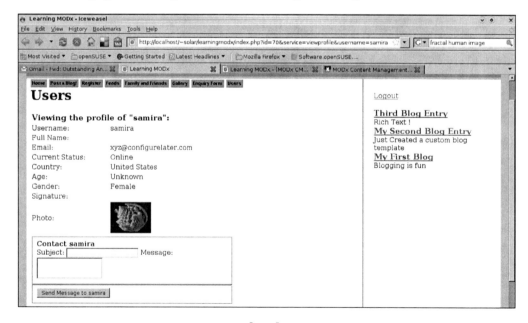

Link to edit profile

Now you have an edited Profile page. For users to be able to access the page, we need to be able to show a link to that page. The link should only appear only when the user is logged in. The snippet `Personalize`, which comes with MODx allows us to do this:

Edit the `Learning MODx` default template to add the highlighted section

```
<!DOCTYPE html PUBLIC "-//W3C//DTD XHTML 1.1//EN" "http://www.w3.org/
TR/xhtml11/DTD/xhtml11.dtd"> <html xmlns="http://www.w3.org/1999/
xhtml" xml:lang="en">
  <head>
    <title>Learning MODx</title>
    <meta http-equiv="Content-Type" content="text/html; charset=iso-
                                                          8859-1" />
    <link rel="stylesheet" type="text/css" href="style.css" />
  </head>
  <body>
    <div id="banner">
      <h1>Learning MODx</h1>

    </div>

    <div id="wrapper">
      <div id="container">
        <div id="content">
          <div id="col-1">
<div id="menu">
[!Wayfinder?startId=`0` &amp;level=`2` &amp;outerClass=`outer`
&amp;innerClass='inner' &amp;lastClass=`last` &amp;firstClass=`first`
&amp;hereClass=`active`!]
</div>
          <h1>[*pagetitle*]</h1>
          <br/>

          [*#content*]
        </div>
        <div id="col-2" >

          <div > [!Personalize?&yesChunk=`profilelink`!]
                            [!WebLogin!]  </div>

            <div>
              [!Ditto? &parents=`47` &tpl=`dittofrontpage`!]
            </div>
```

```
<div>
[!DittoCala?calSource=`64` !]
</div>

        </div>
      </div>
    </div>
    <div class="clearing"> </div>
  </div> <!-- end of wrapper div -->
  <div id="footer">It is fun and exciting to build websites with
                                      MODx</div>
</body>
</html>
```

What we are doing here is telling the `Personalize` snippet to render a chunk call to the `profilelink` if the user is logged in.

Now, let us create the chunk `profilelink` to display the link. Place the following code in the new chunk:

```
<a href="[~71~]">My Profile</a>
```

Replace `71` with whatever is the document ID of your `My Profile` document.

Now the Front Page, if you are logged in, looks like the following:

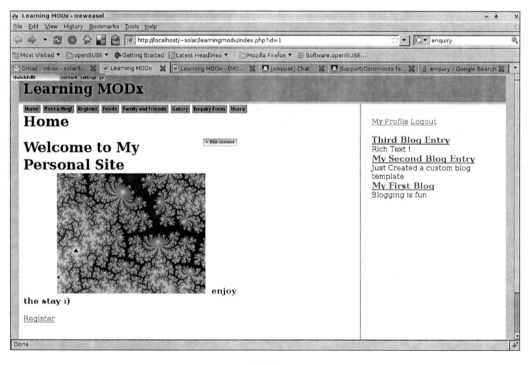

Notice that the link does not appear when you are logged out.

There are many ways to have user profiles in MODx; what we have shown here using `WebLoginPE` is just one of the ways. The other possibilities include associating every new user with a document, and assigning those documents with a template that has the necessary template variables to store the user's data.

Similar posts

It would be a nice feature to show the similar posts from the same category when displaying blog entries. At first thought, it may be tempting to think that we will need to look for a snippet that does this. This example will demonstrate that many functionalities can be implemented by the proper usage of the snippets that you already know. In this case, we will be using the `Ditto` snippet.

The `Ditto` call that has to be included in the `Learning` MODx blog template is:

```
[!Ditto? &parents=`47` &filter=`tvBlogcategories,[*Blogcategories*],7
                                     |id,[*id*],2`!]
```

This section will teach you how we came to get this snippet call step by step. It is important that you learn the process of building a complex snippet call. When the solution for the requirement is approached logically, solving one hurdle at a time, the whole procedure becomes very simple.

We already know that `Ditto` can be used to show all the MODx documents from a particular container. Since all our blogs are in a container with ID 47 (in an earlier chapter, we explained that this ID can be different for you), to display all the blogs, we will call `Ditto` as follows:

```
[!Ditto? &parents=`47`!]
```

We have also learned that we can use filters to display documents with a specific template variable value. This has already been demonstrated when we created RSS feeds for different category of blogs. So a call like

```
[!Ditto? &parents=`47` &filter=`tvBlogcategories, IT, 7`!]
```

...will display all the blogs from the IT category. Now this is fine when we are in a blog page that is also of the IT category. But when we are visiting a blog that is of the sports category, we will want to display blogs from the sports category. So in the filter, instead of IT or `Sports`, we will have to have a variable that changes its value depending on which document is being viewed. Here we can use the template variable of the document itself to achieve this. Hence,

```
[!Ditto? &parents=`47` &filter=`tvBlogcategories,[*Blogcategories*],7
```

will translate to

```
[!Ditto? &parents=`47` &filter=`tvBlogcategories,IT,7
```

in a blog with the category as IT, and to

```
[!Ditto? &parents=`47` &filter=`tvBlogcategories,Sports,7
```

in a blog with the category as Sports.

The snippet call to show the similar posts is almost complete, as we show blogs from the same category. But there is one more enhancement that needs to be done. We don't want the blog page that we are in to be listed in the similar posts as well. Hence, we need to filter out the current document. We already know we can club filters together using the | operator, and also that we can filter documents based on ID. A filtering expression like

```
id,1,2
```

will filter out document 1. What we need is to replace 1 with the current document's ID. So the filter expression will be:

```
id,[*id*],2
```

By clubbing all this together, we get:

```
[!Ditto? &parents=`47` &filter=`tvBlogcategories,[*Blogcategories*],7
                                            |id,[*id*],2`!]
```

We can implement this by modifying the template to contain the following addition. Modify the Learning MODx blog template to the following:

```
<!DOCTYPE html PUBLIC "-//W3C//DTD XHTML 1.1//EN" "http://www.w3.org/
TR/xhtml11/DTD/xhtml11.dtd"> <html xmlns="http://www.w3.org/1999/
xhtml" xml:lang="en">
  <head>
    <title>Learning MODx</title>
    <meta http-equiv="Content-Type" content="text/html; charset=iso-
                                                 8859-1" />
    <link rel="stylesheet" type="text/css" href="style.css" />
  </head>
  <body>
    <div id="banner">
      <h1>Learning MODx</h1>
    </div>

    <div id="wrapper">
      <div id="container">
        <div id="content">
```

```
                <div id="col-1">
<div id="menu">
[!Wayfinder?startId=`0` &amp;level=`2` &amp;outerClass=`outer`
&amp;innerClass='inner' &amp;lastClass=`last` &amp;firstClass=`first`
&amp;hereClass=`active`!]
</div>
                <h1>[*pagetitle*]</h1>
                <br/>

                [*#content*]
<br>
[!Jot? &placeholders=1 &output=0 &tplForm=`comments`
                        &canpost=`Registered Users`!]

<hr/>
[+jot.html.comments+]
[+jot.html.form+]
<hr/>
[+jot.html.moderate+]

        </div>

        <div id="col-2" >
            <div > [!WebLogin!]   </div>

<div>
<h3>Similar Posts in [*Blogcategories*]</h3>

[!Ditto? &parents=`47` &filter=`tvBlogcategories,[*Blogcategories*],7
                                        |id,[*id*],2`!]

</div>
        </div>
      </div>
    </div>
    <div class="clearing"> </div>
  </div> <!-- end of wrapper div -->
  <div id="footer">It is fun and exciting to build websites with
                                        MODx</div></body>
</html>
```

Notice that we have also used the template variable `[*Blogcategories*]` in the caption. Now you can preview a blog and it will look like the following with the new **Related Posts** functionality working.

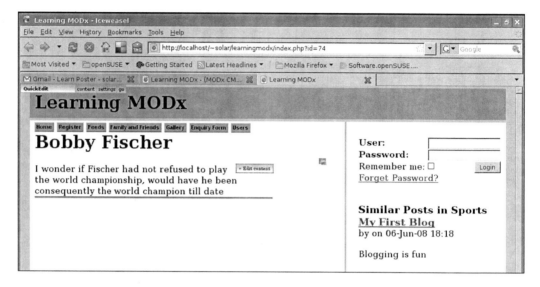

Summary

In this chapter, we have seen how we can use what we have already learned to create:

- Forums with the SMF module
- Image Galleries with MaxiGallery
- Enquiry Forms supporting validation and email with eForms
- User Profiles with WebLoginPe
- Similar Posts with Ditto

We have also seen how we can approach a given requirement logically, step by step, to construct the complex snippet calls that provide the solution. This chapter showcases everything that you have learned so far in quick demonstrations.

11
Creating Snippets

We have so far learned how to use snippets to get the required functionality for our site. What about when there are no snippets available to do what we want to do? We might have to go and create the snippet ourselves. Fortunately, unlike most other CMSs, MODx requires no, or very little, overhead to turn any regular PHP code into a snippet. This chapter requires you to have a basic knowledge of PHP. However, even if this is not the case, it might be helpful to read, as it should clearly reveal to you what is happening in a snippet.

Learning to create a snippet

In this section, we will learn to create a snippet by using a simple 'Hello World' program in PHP. To test the output, we will create a document with the following details:

Field Name	Field Value
Title	Creating a Snippet
Uses template	`Learning MODx default template`
Document content	`[!helloworld!]`
Show in menu	unchecked

From the earlier chapter on using snippets, we have learned that a snippet could do one or more of the following three things:

- Return an HTML output that gets inserted in place of the snippet call
- Create and store values in placeholders, which can later be used in the document/template that called the snippet
- Create and store values in placeholders, and also process a chunk that uses these placeholders and insert the chunk's HTML with the placeholders' values in the document/template that called the snippet

In this section, we will learn how to make any regular PHP code do all of the mentioned things. For this demonstration, we will convert the following PHP code to behave like a snippet.

```php
<?php
echo "Hello World!<br>";
echo "It is a beautiful day";
?>
```

Returning an output

Let us create the snippet Hello World! now.

1. Click on the **Manage Resources** menu in the **Resources** menu.
2. Click on the **Snippets** tab.
3. Click on **New Snippet** and fill in the following details.

Field Name	Field Value
Snippet name	Hello World!
Snippet code	The PHP code above
Existing Category in Properties tab	Learning MODx

4. Click on **Save**.

Now preview the document that you have just created. You will see something like the following:

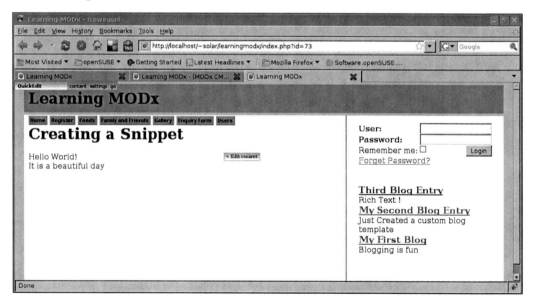

It seems that the snippet is working without any modifications. But this method for showing the message is not recommended, and might have inconsistent behavior. The recommmended method of rendering the output is to keep concatenating whatever has to be shown in a string and finally return the string. Change the code in the Hello World! snippet to the following.

```php
<?php
$message = "Hello World!<br>";
$message .="It is a beautiful day";
return $message;
?>
```

Now preview the document and notice that the output has not changed and is the same as the previous screenshot. The only change is that you have used the recommended method to display the same output.

To summarize what you have just learned — whatever you finally return using the return keyword gets shown in the place of the snippet call. We can use this behavior by concatenating all that we want to be shown as the output in a single variable and finally returning it.

Returning placeholders

Now that we have seen how to display an output in place of the snippet call, we will learn how we can create placeholders instead. We will also learn that the user has the flexibility to use the placeholders anywhere in the document. What basically happens here is this: we decide that we want to have a certain placeholder, we create it in the snippet and assign it a value, the placeholder is inserted after the snippet call in the document, and the document shows the value of the placeholder.

To create a placeholder and assign a value to it, we use the MODx function $MODx->setPlaceholder.

The function accepts two parameters — the name of the placeholder and its value. Hence, the syntax is $MODx->setPlaceholder(placeholdername, value);.

Now let us modify our snippet to use placeholders using what we have just learned.

Modify the snippet code to the following:

```php
<?php
$MODx->setPlaceholder("message1", "Hello World!");
$MODx->setPlaceholder("message2","It is a beautiful day");
return;
?>
```

Note that we could have just created one placeholder with the name *message* and the value as $message. We have created two, just to demonstrate how placeholders can be placed anywhere in the document.

To test the results, we also need to modify the **Create a Snippet** document to use the placeholders. Change the content of the MODx document to the following:

```
[!helloworld!]
Before Placeholder1 <br>
[+message1+] <br>
Before Placeholder2 <br>
[+message2+]
```

Now preview the document and it will look like the following:

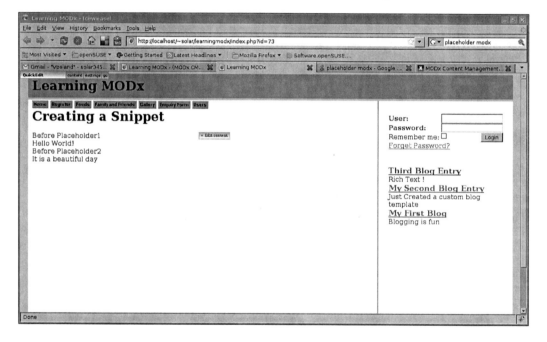

The next diagram will illustrate the flow:

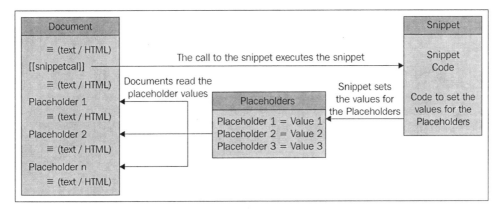

Processing a chunk

From the previous example, we had the following in the document:

```
Before Placeholder1 <br>
[+message1+] <br>
Before Placeholder2 <br>
[+message2+]
```

It is possible to isolate this from the document, and hence make the code even cleaner to maintain. We can do this by placing this code in a chunk and making the snippet call this chunk. Let us try this by doing the following:

Change the document code to:

```
[!helloworld!]
```

Create a chunk with `helloworld` with the following content:

```
Before Placeholder1 <br>
[+message1+] <br>
Before Placeholder2 <br>
[+message2+]
```

Change the snippet code to the following:

```
<?php
$MODx->setPlaceholder('message1', "Hello World!");
$MODx->setPlaceholder("message2","It is a beautiful day");
$output = $MODx->getChunk("helloworld");
return $output;
?>
```

If you preview the page, it will look like the previous screenshot. What has changed is the way that we have implemented the same thing. It is cleaner and easier to maintain using chunks.

The following diagram illustrates the flow:

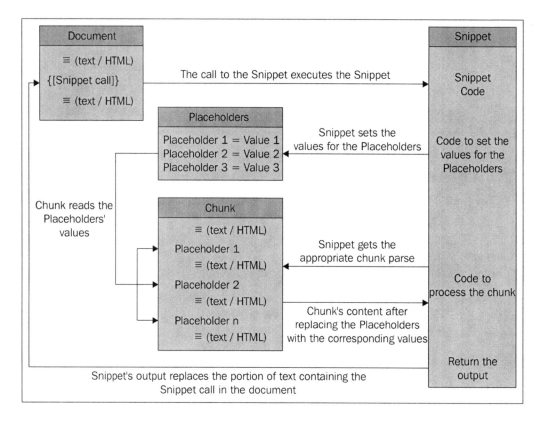

Note that this example is using only one chunk to demonstrate the concept of chunks. A snippet can use multiple chunks as well, if there is a necessity to do so.

Using parameters

Now that we have made our snippet create placeholders and then use a chunk for rendering the output, it would be nice if we could make our snippet more flexible. What if it could use any chunk instead of a predefined `helloworld` chunk to render the output? This might be necessary if you want to call the same snippet two times in the same page, and if you want a different output or style for each call. To make this possible, we will need to be able to get the chunk name from the snippet call. This can be done using parameters. Using parameters in a call, we can pass the snippet values that it can use. For this example, we will use a parameter called `&tpl`. The snippet will check if the call to it has any value for `tpl`. If it does, then it will use that value as the chunk name; if it doesn't exist, it will use `helloworld` as the chunk name. This way the snippet has a sensible default value and yet provides a mechanism to override it.

To see the use of parameters, change the `helloworld` snippet code to the following

```
<?php
$tpl = (isset($tpl))? $tpl : 'helloworld';
$MODx->setPlaceholder('message1', "Hello World!");
$MODx->setPlaceholder("message2","It is a beautiful day");
$output = $MODx->getChunk($tpl);
return $output;
?>
```

Notice that the parameters from the document/template are available as regular variables within the snippet. We are using a ternary operator to set the value of `$tpl` to `helloworld` here, if there was no custom value passed along with the call.

Modify the document created earlier, titled `testing snippet`, to contain the following:

```
[!helloworld?&tpl=`helloworldx`!]
```

Create a new chunk called `helloworldx` with the following content:

```
This is from chunk helloworldx<br>

Before Placeholder1 <br>
[+message1+] <br>
Before Placeholder2 <br>
[+message2+]
```

Now preview the document; it will look like the following:

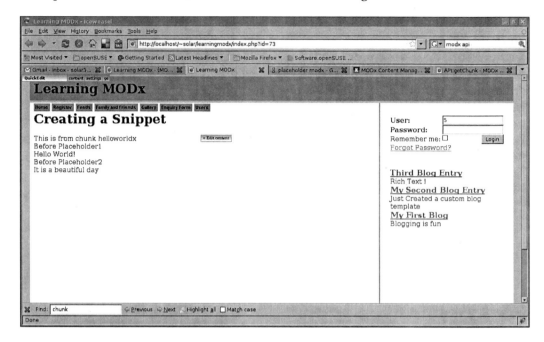

Notice that this call to the snippet used the chunk `helloworldx` instead of the `helloworld` chunk.

MODx API

MODx provides APIs that you can use to avoid recreating commonly used functions. The MODx APIs are accessed through the DocumetParser object $MODx. You can explore more of the MODx internals by trying the following at the top of the `helloworld` snippet:

```
echo '<pre>';
print_r($MODx);
echo '</pre>';
exit;
```

This will print the entire structure of the $MODx object, so you can learn a great deal from the output.

You can use any of the available API functions from within the snippet using `$MODx->functionname()` syntax. In fact, the functions you have been using to set the placeholders, and to display a chunk, are themselves part of the MODx API that is available through the `$MODx` object.

We will see examples of a few of them next.

For example:

- `$MODx->getDocument(1)` will get all of the fields of document 1.
- `$MODx->getAllChildren(1)` will get all of the child documents of document 1.
- `$MODx->getTemplateVars` will return an array of all of the template variables that the template for the current document is using.

DBAPI

The DBAPI is a sub-class of the DocumentParser. It provides a glue between the database and the PHP code in MODx. Using these functions instead of the PHP database functions will allow you to write code that doesn't have to be specific for any database. The following is a list of a few DBAPI functions. When using DBAPI, you will be using the `$table_prefix` variable, which will give the prefix to the table including the database name. This again ensures that you don't have to worry about migration issues, when moving the site using your snippet to another location with a new database name.

$MODx->db->select

Syntax: `select([string $fields [, string $from [, string $where [, string $orderby [, string $limit]]]]])` —can be used for executing an SQL query. All arguments except `$from` are optional.

Parameters:

- `$fields` are the field or column name(s) that you want returned. If they are left blank, they will default to all (`*`).
- `$from` is the table to query. If it is left blank, function will return false
- `$where` is the full string of the WHERE clause of the mySQL query. Leave blank to do no WHERE matching.
- `$orderby`, if needed, can either be ASC or DESC.
- `$limit` is the limit of the number of results to return; leave blank for all.

For example:

```
$res = $MODx->db->select("", $table_prefix.".MODx_site_content",
                                "parent = 10", "ASC" , 10);
```

This will get ten records in ascending order that have the value `10` for the field `parent` from the table `MODx_site_content`.

$MODx->db->getRecordCount

Syntax: `getRecordCount ($resultset)` — retrieves the number of rows from a result set.

Parameter:

- `$resultset` — any result set that is a returned by the usage of `select` or `show`

For example:

```
$count = $MODx->db->getRecordCount ($res);
```

If the result set `$res` has five records, `$count` will be `5`.

$MODx->db->makeArray

Syntax: `makeArray($resultset )` — will convert a result set into an multidimensional array.

Parameters:

- `$resultset` — any result set that is returned by the usage of select or show

For example:

```
$resultsarr = $MODx->db->makeArray($resultset);
```

`$resultarr` will contain a multidimensional array representation of the result set.

Fortunes

Now that you have learned how snippets are created, we will create a snippet that displays a random fortune from the database. Fortunes are just quotations from famous texts, like quotes of the day. They are called fortunes in the UNIX culture, after the introduction of the command-line program called *fortune* many decades ago.

Creating the table

We will create a table that will hold the fortune and the author's name, using phpmyadmin, to keep it simple. Most snippets that use a custom table will automatically create the table if it doesn't already exist.

1. Open phpMyAdmin. The URL for phpMyAdmin will be different depending on your method of installation. If you choose to install Apache and PHP individually, then you will have to install phpMyAdmin first. If you are using XAMPP, as explained in the second chapter, then the URL is `http://localhost/phpmyadmin`.

2. Log in using the username mySQL and the password that you created initially.

3. Click on the `learningMODx` table.

4. At the bottom of the page, under the heading **Create New Table**, name the table `MODx_fortunes` and set **Number of fields** as **3**.

5. Give the following values for the fields.

Field	Type	Length	Extra	Primary Key
id	INT		**Auto Increment**	Checked
text	VARCHAR	255		
author	VARCHAR	100		

Insert a few fortune records, such as:

It's hard to read through a book on the principles of magic without glancing at the cover periodically to make sure it isn't a book on software design – Bruce Tognazzini

Debugging is twice as hard as writing the code in the first place. Therefore, if you write the code as cleverly as possible, you are, by definition, not smart enough to debug it. – Brian Kernighan

No emotion, any more than a wave, can long retain its own individual form – Henry Ward Beecher

Code for fortunes

We now have a table with the records that contain fortunes. The following is the snippet code that displays a random fortune:

```php
<?php
$res = $MODx->db->select("*", $table_prefix."MODx_fortunes"); // Fetch
all the records from the table
$count = $MODx->db->getRecordCount( $res); // Get the total number of
records
if($count==0)
{
return "There are no Fortunes";
}
$x = rand(0,$count-1); // Get a random number between 0 and record
                                                              count
$fortunes = $MODx->db->makeArray($res); // Convert the recordset to
                                                        an array
$fortune = $fortunes[$x]; // Get the nth record where n is the random
                                                            number
$o = '<h3>Fortune</h3>';
$o .= $fortune["text"];
$o .= "<br>";
$o .= $fortune['author'];
return $o;
?>
```

The preceding code queries the table for all the records using the MODx DBAPI, from which we get the number of records. Then a random number is generated from 0 to a count less than the number of records, and we pick the record after converting the result set to an array using the random number as the index. We could also have used the rand() function in the SQL query with LIMIT 1 to get a random record, but since the name of the function is different across MySQL and PostgreSQL, we would have to implement the database-specific code.

Now create a snippet with the following details:

Field Name	Field Value
Snippet name	Fortunes
Snippet Code	The preceding code
Existing Category	Learning MODx

Testing the snippet

Let's test the snippet by calling it from the Learning MODx default template. Modify the template code of the Learning MODx default template to:

```
<!DOCTYPE html PUBLIC "-//W3C//DTD XHTML 1.1//EN" "http://www.w3.org/
TR/xhtml11/DTD/xhtml11.dtd"> <html xmlns="http://www.w3.org/1999/
xhtml" xml:lang="en">
 <head>
  <title>Learning MODx</title>
  <meta http-equiv="Content-Type" content="text/html; charset=iso-
                                        8859-1" />
  <link rel="stylesheet" type="text/css" href="style.css" />
 </head>
 <body>
  <div id="banner">
   <h1>Learning MODx</h1>

  </div>

  <div id="wrapper">
   <div id="container">
   <div id="content">
    <div id="col-1">
<div id="menu">
[!Wayfinder?startId=`0` &amp;level=`2` &amp;outerClass=`outer`
&amp;innerClass='inner' &amp;lastClass=`last` &amp;firstClass=`first`
&amp;hereClass=`active`!]
</div>

      <h1>[*pagetitle*]</h1>
      <br/>

      [*#content*]
      </div>

     <div id="col-2" >

     <div> [!fortunes!] </div>

      <div > [!Personalize?&yesChunk=`profilelink`!] [!WebLogin!]
                                                      </div>

        <div>
        [!Ditto? &parents=`47` &tpl=`dittofrontpage`!]
        </div>

<div>
[!DittoCala?calSource=`64` !]
</div>
```

```
        </div>
      </div>
      </div>
      <div class="clearing"> </div>
    </div> <!-- end of wrapper div -->
    <div id="footer">It is fun and exciting to build websites with
                                         MODx</div></body>
  </html>
```

Now you can preview the Front Page and it will appear like the following:

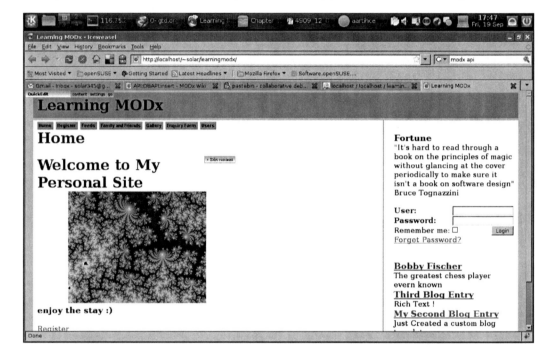

Refresh the page to check if you get another fortune.

Chunks, placeholders, and parameters

We have now got the fortune snippet working, so let us enhance it. We can do the following improvements on it:

- Create placeholders for the fortune text and the author
- Define a parameter to specify a chunk name
- Process the output using the given chunk

We have already seen how to do all of these things in the Hello World! example.

To create placeholders:

```
$MODx->setPlaceholder('fortunetext',$fortune["text"]);
$MODx->setPlaceholder('fortuneauthor',$fortune["author"]);
```

To accept parameters for the output template:

```
$tpl = (isset($tpl))? $tpl : 'fortune';
```

To process the output using the given chunk:

```
$o = $MODx->getChunk($tpl);
```

Hence, the final snippet of code will be:

```
<?php
$tpl = (isset($tpl))? $tpl : 'fortunes';
$res = $MODx->db->select("*", $table_prefix."MODx_fortunes"); //
                         Fetch all the records from the table
$count = $MODx->db->getRecordCount( $res); // Get the total number of
                                                            records
$x = rand(0,$count-1); // Get a random number between 0 and record
                                                            count
$fortunes = $MODx->db->makeArray($res); // Convert the recordset to
                                                        an array
$fortune = $fortunes[$x]; // Get the nth record where n is the random
                                                        number
$MODx->setPlaceholder('fortunetext',$fortune["text"]);
$MODx->setPlaceholder('fortuneauthor',$fortune["author"]);
$o = $MODx->getChunk($tpl);
return $o;
?>
```

Modify the `fortune` snippet to contain the preceding code.

Now, you will have to create a chunk for the snippet to use. As we are not passing any parameter in the snippet call, it will use the chunk named `fortunes`. So let us create a chunk with the following details:

Field Name	Field Value
Chunk name	fortunes
Existing Category	Learning MODx
Chunk code	`<h3>Fortune</h3>`
	`[+fortunetext+]`
	` `
	`[+fortuneauthor+]`

Now preview the Front Page again. You should be able to see the fortune just as before.

Using files

It is also possible that you will have a large snippet that is split into multiple files. In such a case, you will still have to create a snippet the way we have learned above. The other files can be included from within the snippet; for example, to include a file for the fortune snippet, the line of code could be:

```
include MODX_BASE_PATH.'assets/snippets/fortunes/lib.php';
```

MODX_BASE_PATH stores the base directory of the installation.

The convention followed when using external files is to place them in a directory with the name of the snippet inside assets/snippets.

Summary

In this chapter, you have learned how to create snippets, the different ways of displaying the output, and how to implement them. You have also learned to use the available MODx APIs, and why you should use them. You have created a new snippet for the site that displays a random fortune. The snippet accepts a parameter and displays the output using chunks and placeholders. You finally learned how snippets can use files like libraries.

12
SEO, Deployment, and Security

In this chapter, we will discuss all that you need to take care of once you have developed the site. We will discuss how MODx helps you to take your site to the top of the search ladder, and then we will deal with deployment and keeping your site secured.

SEO

We all know **Search Engine Optimization (SEO)** is about getting a better rank in the search engines like Google, so that your site comes towards the top of the results list when someone searches for the content that is available in your site. In this section, we will discuss the various factors that contribute to getting a site optimized for a search engine, and also discuss what MODx provides to make it possible.

Search engine-friendly URLs

Clean URLs are URLs without the ugly `?=xxxxxxxxxx` at the end. This format is used to pass parameters to a page by appending a `?` and a key (`=`) value pair to the URL. For example, to pass `id = 7` to the `index.php` page, the URL might look like `http://localhost/learningMODx/index.php?id=7`. If you observe closely, you will notice that whatever document you want to visit, MODx is actually calling the `index.php` page with the ID of the respective document ID as a parameter. Almost all CMSs behave in the same way. All CMSs execute only one PHP page, which in turn parses the required document. Friendlier URLs mean that instead of using the URL `http://localhost/learningMODx/index.php?id=7`, we would want the URL to look like `http://localhost/learningMODx/7`. This URL appears friendlier, not just to the end users, but also to machines. If you would like to find out more about how this appears friendly to machines, you might want to Google for 'REST' and read about it. Now that this URL appears friendlier to machines, there are higher chances that it is ranked higher. MODx supports clean URLs.

To turn on clean URLs, you must first have `mod_rewrite` loaded to Apache.

If you are using Apache with XAMPP, as explained in Chapter 2, then this feature is on by default. Alternatively, if you are using Apache from any Debian-based distro, you can load the module by:

```
a2enmod rewrite
apache2ctl restart
```

What essentially happens when using the `rewrite` module is that there is a file in the MODx directory called `.htaccess` that contains rules on how to translate the URL. So, although the requested URL is `http://localhost/learningMODx/7`, the `rewrite` module of Apache after reading the configuration file will translate it to `http://localhost/learningMODx/index.php?id=7`. You can also manually edit the `ht.access` file to give new rules of mapping if you like.

You will find a file with the name `ht.access` in the MODx root directory. Rename this file as `.htaccess`. Do the same thing with the `ht.access` file in the `manager` directory.

Now, open the `.htaccess` file in the MODx root directory and edit the line `RewriteBase /` to contain the `MODxfolderpath`, which in our case is `learningMODx`. Hence you will have to change the mentioned line to `RewriteBase /learningMODx`.

If you are editing this file in Windows, make sure that the editor does not save any alien character. It is preferable not to use WordPad, Word, Dreamweaver, or anything of that sort to edit the configuration files to avoid this happening.

Configure the **Friendly URLs** page in the Manager interface to meet your requirements. MODx makes it easier for you to configure the mapping of a URL to a friendly name pattern that you prefer.

The following is a screenshot of the configuration page for **Friendly URLs**. You can get to this page by clicking on **Configuration** on the **Tools** menu and then selecting the **Friendly URLs** tab.

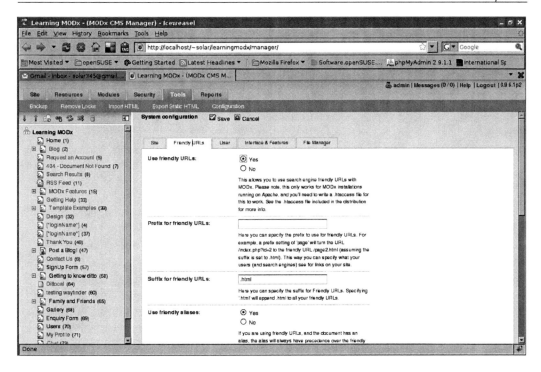

Change the **Use friendly URLs** option to **Yes** and click **Save**.

Now you can go to the main page `http://localhost/learningMODx` and open any page using the menu. You will notice that the links have changed to be more friendly, with the form `http://localhost/learningMODx/pageid.html`.

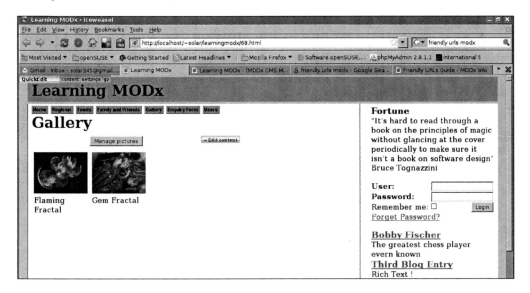

You can go ahead and change the prefix and suffix. By default, the prefix is blank and the suffix is `.html`, and that is the reason you get `pageid.html`. I like to leave the `.html` prefix blank too. This means you will have `http://localhost/learningMODx/pageid`.

The next option on the page is the **Use friendly aliases** option. When this option is turned on, the page can be accessed using the alias name instead of the ID. Our Home Page has the ID 1. Let us give it an alias. In the Friendly URLs configuration page, turn **Alias** to **On** and remove the `.html` suffix. Now try opening the URL `http:/localhost/learningMODx/home`. You will see the Home Page. With the **Use alias** option, it is possible to access the documents by a name instead of a number.

The next option is the **Use friendly alias path**, which will make a document accessible by its full path. Supposing the document is a child of a container document and both these documents have an alias, then the document can be accessed by `http://localhost/learningMODx/parentalias/childalias`. Note that turning this option on would require you to turn the next option — **Allow duplicate aliases** — on, which is not recommended. Duplicate aliases mean that a document can be accessed by more than one alias. This introduces an SEO problem. A site is more optimized for searching if every page has only one corresponding URL. That is, to access a particular page, there must be only one URL. This is known as *Canonicalization*. To make this happen, you can use the SEO Strict plug-in that will only allow the documents to be accessed by the exact alias. The next option is **Automatically generate alias**; turning this option on will automatically generate page aliases from the title of the page. Of course, you can still edit the generated aliases in case you want a different alias for a particular page.

Meta tags and keywords

Meta tags are a way for you to define what your web site is about, to the outside world. These tags are generally placed within the `<head>` tag. Meta tags are specified using the `<meta> </meta>` tags. These tags have two attributes: `name` and `content`. The `name` attribute is used to specify the name of the element and the `content` attribute specifies the value for that element. For example:

```
<meta name="description" content="MODx reference">
```

There are a set of defined elements such as `author` and `description`. Setting these elements makes your site description clearer, and hence it will have a higher chance of getting a better rating. There is also an element called `keyword`, which can contain a list of space-separated words. The keyword element is used to inform the search engine about what content to expect in the site. Hence, setting the meta tags and keywords should make the site more search-engine optimized.

MODx comes with a Manager interface to add meta tags and keywords to the entire site. To access this page:

1. Click on the **Manage Resources** on the **Resource** menu.
2. Click on **Manage META** tags and **Keywords**.

You will see a screen like the following:

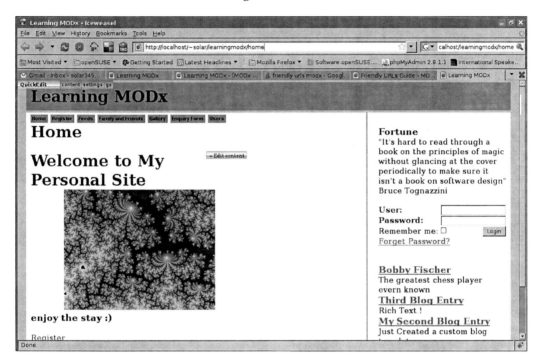

Here you can add, edit, and delete tags and keywords. This is rarely used, since the process for specifying keywords for individual documents is rather cumbersome. Most people use a TV to assign the keywords, and then in their template have the meta tag with the TV tag in place of a list of keywords. This way, you can easily edit the TV field for each document.

Site map

A site map is an XML page that lets the search engines know the layout of your site. Generally, you will have to create it yourself. But MODx has a snippet that does it automatically for you.

To use the snippet, perform the following steps:

1. Download the snippet from `http://MODxcms.com/sitemap-711.html`.

2. To install the snippet, click on **Create new snippet** in the **Resource Manager** and paste the code from the downloaded file.

3. Give the snippet the name `SiteMap`. (More instructions on installing snippets can be found in Chapter 8.)

4. Create a document with the following details.

Field Name	Field Value
Title	SiteLayout
Uses template	(blank)
Content Type	text/xml
Document content	`[!SiteMap? &format=`sp`!]`

5. Preview the SiteLayout page and you will see something like the following which contains a description of the entire site.

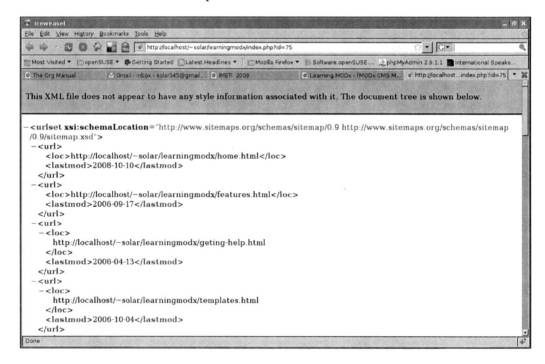

> **SiteMap Parameters**
> Google has a feature where you can check individual pages using the site layout. You can do this by using the service provided by Google at http://www.google.com/webmasters/tools/.

XHTML Strict

It is good practice to use XHTML Strict conventions. This does make a difference in SEO. Unlike HTML, all XHTML tags have to be closed, and it is sometimes difficult to make a page XHTML-complaint when there is a lot of code mixed with it. Since MODx allows you to keep templates as plain XHTML with only variable replacements and snippet calls, it is easier in MODx to maintain XHTML strict compliance. You can always validate any page for complete compliance at http://validator.w3.org/.

Other SEO tweaks

In this section, we will quickly list a few other SEO tricks that aren't specific to MODx.

Using CSS to control the layout

Always use CSS to control the layout and don't mix it with the content.

Content first

Always have the content as close to the `<body>` tag as possible. In the case of a site with large drop-down menus, have them placed in the bottom and use CSS to move them up.

Hidden text

Search engines, such as Google, consider hidden text to be misleading and remove such pages from indexing. Always make sure that you don't have text that machines can read but humans can't. An example would be a text box with size set to 1 pixel. When search engines encounter such pages, they tend to believe that you are trying to mislead the search.

Descriptive text

Always have descriptive texts for the images, flash scripts, and any other objects that you embed. It not only helps people who use a screen reader to understand the contents of the site, but also makes such content known to the search engines.

Tracking

Use a tracking mechanism to monitor the changes in hit ratio. Once you are aware of what works and what doesn't for your site, you will be able to tune it better. An example of such a tracking service is Google analytics.

Inbound links

The more people link to your site, the more likely your site will appear on the top of the list. Get more people to refer to your site. Somehow this trend is picking up with the blogging community so rapidly that we are left with learning from them!

Quality content

Have quality content in your site. Quality content is not just what you have, it is also how you have structured it and placed it. With appropriate headings and relevant references, you are more likely to get a higher number of hits.

Deployment

Once you have completed the development of your web site, you will want to make it available to the whole world. For this, you will have to deploy the web site in a web server connected to the Internet. Any server that can run PHP and MYSQL is suitable for MODx, and you can get an account starting from $3 a month. In this section, we will discuss what you need to move the web site from one computer to another

Filesystem

When migrating the web site, you will have to copy the MODx installation root directory to the appropriate directory in your web server. There is nothing much that can go wrong in this process. Just make sure that all of the files are copied. Also, the transferred files may have different permissions on the new server. In such a case, the site will throw an error indicating the file permissions. If that happens, change the permissions accordingly as described in Chapter 2.

Depending on your hosting provider, you will be given one of the following ways of transferring files. There is an excellent full backup module that will zip up the whole filesystem as well as back up the database as a single ZIP file. You can then usually simply upload the ZIP file and unzip it using the site control panel's *File Management* feature. The extracted folder will contain a file with the .sql extension. You can import the database with this file using phpMyAdmin, or any other database management interface the hosting service provides.

FTP

FTP is one of the most commonly used protocols to transfer the files.

To get FTP on Windows, download the program called **winscp** from
`http://winscp.net`.

Open it and fill in the **User name** and **password** that you have been given by your
hosting provider. Enter the domain name, and choose the **Protocol** as **FTP**.

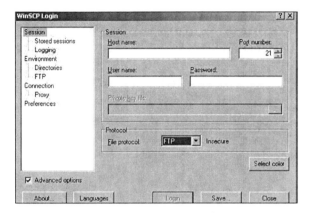

Click on **Connect**. You will see two panes. The left pane shows the files in your local
machine and the right side shows the files in the remote machine:

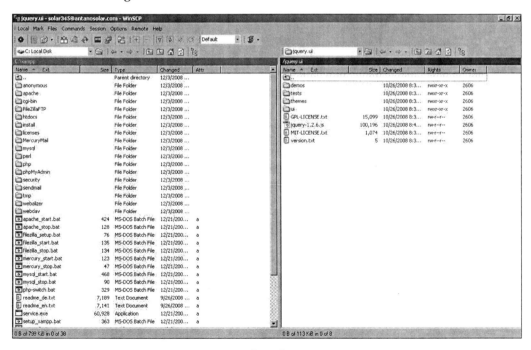

In Linux, you can use the `ftp` command to connect to the FTP server. Give your username and password when asked. (For example: `ftp antanosolar.com`)

The `put` command helps you to transfer files from the local machine to the remote machine.

To transfer all the files and folders within a folder, you can use the `-r` parameter. Just like regular file systems, wild cards are accepted. `*` means all the files and `xyz*` means all the files starting with `xyz`.

For example, `put * -r` will transfer all the files and folders recursively.

The `get` command is used to transfer the files from the remote server to the local machine. It behaves in a similar way to `put`.

Alternatively, you can use a GUI-based client such as **kasablanca** or **kftpgrabber**. There is also another program called **curl**, which is worth trying. Curl can work over multiple protocols and is the preferred way among those who use Linux for their day-to-day activities.

SFTP

To install on Windows, follow the same steps as in the case of FTP, but choose SFTP as the protocol instead of FTP.

In Linux, there are two easy ways to transfer the files between the remote machine and the local machine using SFTP.

You can either get familiar with the `scp` functionality—which is very similar to `cp` that is used for copying files locally, or you can mount the remote file system locally and transfer files to and fro as you will do from a regular file system using `sshfs`. It would be diverging from the topic to explain both `scp` and `sshfs`. We will give you a few pointers here, which can help you learn more.

`scp` is similar to `cp`. You have to specify two arguments: source and destination. If you want to copy a file named `index.php` from the local machine in the current directory to the remote machine, you will use the following command:

`scp index.php username@remotemachineaddress:/foldername`

Similarly, to transfer files from a remote machine to the local machine, you will use:

`scp username@remotemachineaddress:/foldername localpath`

`sshfs` is similar to `mount`. The only difference is that instead of mounting a local file system, you are mounting a remote file system. For this, you will need to first install `sshfs`. The general syntax is:

sshfs `username@remotemachineaddress:`**/foldername /mountfoldername**

You can alternatively use the application SecPanel, which has a GUI for `scp`.

WebDAV

WebDAV was originally meant for collaborative authoring, though these days it is also used for sharing files. WebDAV operates over the HTTP protocol. It is sometimes referred to as DAV for short. To use a DAV resource:

In Windows:

1. Open **My Network Places**.
2. Click on **Add Network Place**.
3. Click on **Choose another network location**.
4. Enter the given URL from the service provider followed by the username and password in the Internet or network address box.
5. Now you will be able to access your files from **My Network Places**.

In Linux, the procedure to use a DAV resource is similar to mounting a filesystem over SFTP. You need to install an application called **fusedav**, and then you can mount the filesystem locally. `fusedav` has the following syntax:

```
fusedav remoteurl /mountfoldername
```

Database

MODx stores all the documents and templates that you create in the database. So you will have to transfer the database as well for your site to be deployed. Almost all the hosting providers provide phpMyAdmin to manage the databases. There are two steps to migrating a database

1. Export the database from the local machine.
2. Import the database to the remote machine.

Exporting

To export the database, you can use phpMyAdmin. We have already discussed installation of phpMyAdmin in the second chapter.

1. Log in to phpMyAdmin using the MySQL username and password that you created for the database earlier by opening the URL `http://localhost/ phpmyadmin` in a browser.

2. You will see a list of databases in the server. Click on the database that you want to export.

3. Click on **Export**.

4. Select on the **Save to file** checkbox and click **Go**.

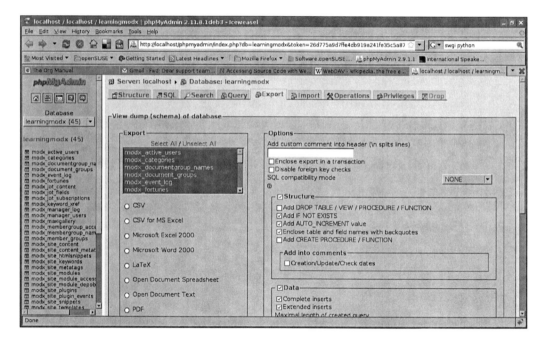

Importing

When you export a database, the default option is to save it as SQL, which means that the exported file has SQL instructions to reconstruct all the tables and records. Of course, you can choose different formats and even have them compressed before exporting. Once you have exported, you will want to import it to the remote server provided by your service provider.

1. Log in to phpMyAdmin using the username as mySQL and the password that was given to you by your service provider.

2. Create a new database, or select a database if you have already created one.

3. Click on **Import**.
4. Click **Browse** and select the file that was exported before.
5. Click on **Go** to import the database.

There is generally a server limitation on the size of the file that can be uploaded. The import screen shows the maximum size that can be uploaded. If the export file is larger than what your service provider allows you to import, try choosing a compression format to reduce the size. The compression works really well, and reduces the size of the exported file by a good ratio. Make sure that the compression format you choose when exporting is also supported by the server in which you are importing. When you click on **Import**, it shows the various compression formats it supports. **Bzip2** is known to offer the highest compression among the various compression formats that are supported.

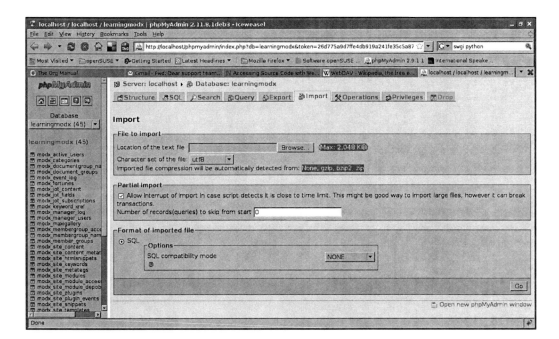

Configuration file

Sometimes you may not be able to use the same name for the database in the new server. Maybe the name is already taken. In such a case, it is alright to give a new database name, username, and password. You will have to make sure that you make the appropriate changes in the `manager/includes/config.inc.php` file and upload it back to the server.

```php
/**
 *      MODx Configuration file
 */
$database_type = 'mysql';
$database_server = 'localhost';
$database_user = 'root';
$database_password = '';
$database_connection_charset = '';
$dbase = 'learningmodx';
$table_prefix = 'modx_';
error_reporting(E_ALL & ~E_NOTICE);

$lastInstallTime = 1211112170;

$site_sessionname = 'SN48301aea4d284';
$https_port = '443';

// automatically assign base_path and base_url
if(empty($base_path)||empty($base_url)||$_REQUEST['base_path']||$_REQUEST['base_url']) {
    $sapi= 'undefined';
    if (!strstr($_SERVER['PHP_SELF'], $_SERVER['SCRIPT_NAME']) && ($sapi= @ php_sapi_name()) == 'cgi') {
        $script_name= $_SERVER['PHP_SELF'];
    } else {
        $script_name= $_SERVER['SCRIPT_NAME'];
    }
    $a= explode("/manager", str_replace("\\", "/", dirname($script_name)));
    if (count($a) > 1)
        array_pop($a);
    $url= implode("manager", $a);
    reset($a);
```

Configurations

Depending on the path of the new location, you might also want to change the following settings in the Manager by clicking on the **Tools** menu and selecting **Configuration**.

- **Resource** path in **Interface & Features**
- **File Manager** path in **File Manager**

 If you had created other Managers' accounts, it may also be necessary to edit these fields for them individually.

Security

In this section, we will discuss the permissions on file systems that have to be set to make sure your site is safe. Also, we will discuss **captcha** and the **mod_security** module for Apache that can cause certain issues arising from security concerns and how to solve them. When using a content management server, unless you are writing snippets yourself, there is nothing much to worry about. There are a few things to keep in mind though, for MODx, and they are mentioned next.

File permissions

It is a good practice to set read-only permissions on all the files except folders that will be updated by MODx. In Linux, you can do this by chmod 0644 * -R within the MODx directory. Some folders must be made writable using chmod 0755 folder name. The following is a list of such folders:

- assets/cache
- assets/files
- assets/media

When you are using an external snippet, and it requires storing files in a separate folder, make sure you make those files writable too. For example, the gallery snippet we saw earlier requires that the folder assets/galleries is writable. More details on what chmod does are explained in Chapter 2.

Installer

The MODx installer files are stored in the install directory. Make sure to delete this folder after installation. Leaving it on the system poses a security risk, and someone may try to install MODx on your system again.

Writable configuration file

MODx stores the configurations of the site in manager/includes/config.inc.php. This file contains the database connection details and other settings. Though during installation this file has to be made writable as MODx will have to store the settings that you enter in the web page, after the installation is complete, you must make it read-only to have a secured site.

Captcha

Captcha is a technology to prevent spam bots. There are malicious machines on the Internet that have programs that can automatically register and post to blogs, and so on. Such programs are called **bots**. Captcha shows an image containing embedded text and asks the user to enter the same in a textbox. This makes sure that the person filling the form, or registering, is a human and not an automated machine. Most MODx snippets that accept input from the user have captcha ability. Make sure you use captcha wherever necessary and make your site spam free.

mod_security

Apache has a security module that checks for code in POST requests and blocks it, which means, if you are adding a snippet using the Manager and submit the form, there are chances that the code may be considered unsafe. In such a case, the snippet will not get saved. In such situations, you can disable the security module for the duration of the post. In a hosted server, this may not be possible. What you can do in hosted servers is write a few additions to the .htaccess file that will permit the data transfer.

You can try one of the following two lines in the .htaccess file:

- To turn off post data filtering:

  ```
  SecFilterScanPOST Off
  ```

- To turn off the security filter engine:

  ```
  SecFilterEngine Off
  ```

Unused files

A recent security exploit demonstrated that unused .php files should never be left in the filesystem. They should either be deleted or renamed (such as the .php files that are included with snippets, plug-ins, and so on, that contain the code to be copied into the Manager). This experience will also most likely teach the snippet authors to name their Manager code files with a different suffix as well, even if this does prevent an editor's syntax coloring from working properly on the file.

Manager configurations

Besides the preceding mentioned security issues, there are simple configurations in the Manager that can help you make your site even more secure. These options can be found when clicking on **Configurations** in the **Tools** menu.

User tab

The following are the options that the User tab supports:

- **Failed Login Attempts**: This option specifies how many times to allow a user to enter a wrong username or password consecutively before blocking the user. This can be useful to prevent a brute force attack, where a program, or even a person, is trying to guess the password of another user.

- **Blocked Minutes**: This option specifies how many minutes to block the user for before allowing login again.

File Manager tab

New File Permissions: Here you can mention the default permissions for the files that are being uploaded. 0644 is safe, and it is the default permission. This makes sure that the files are not writable and executable by everyone.

New Folder Permissions: Here you can set the default permissions for the new folders that you create using the File Manager. The default permission—0755—again, is a very safe option.

Uploadable File Types: In this textbox, you can specify a list of comma-separated file extensions that can be uploaded to the site. It is important that you specify non-executable extensions. It is a good idea to only allow extensions that you are anticipating; for example, if you want to allow the uploading of images, only then you can give the list of .gif, .jpeg, .tif.

Summary

In this chapter, we discussed how to make the site optimized for search engines. We discussed clean URLs, meta tags, site maps, and other tweaks. Having developed the site in a local machine, we learned in this chapter how to deploy it to a remote server. And finally, we looked into what has to be done to make your MODx site secure.

13
Plug-ins and Modules

This chapter explains plug-ins and modules including those that we have used in our application. The chapter will also cover events and plug-in configuration.

Plug-ins and events

Plug-ins are PHP code blocks in MODx that, unlike snippets, are not called for execution from a document or a template. Rather, plug-ins are executed on the trigger of certain events during the document parsing or the other internal processing. Every action in MODx, such as rendering a document, or deleting a user from the system, will trigger a series of flags. Each flag is viewed as an event. For example, you have events such as:

- `OnDocFormPrerender` — triggered just before the document is going to be rendered
- `OnUserFormSave` — triggered just before the user details are saved

There are many such events, and we will not describe each one of them in this chapter. But rather, we will discuss how to write plug-ins that get executed on specific events. We will also describe how to generate events, even custom ones, when you are writing snippets.

We will start by first examining some plug-ins that are already available, if they were installed during the MODx installation, and gradually move into creating a very basic plug-in.

Using an existing plug-in

You can view all of the available plug-ins by clicking on **Resources | Manage resources | Plugins** (as shown next).

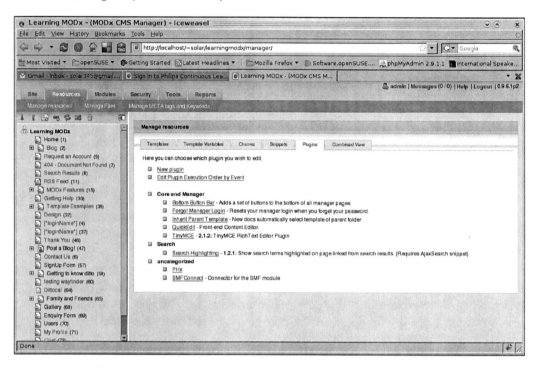

You will notice that PHx—which we used earlier—is also a plug-in. Click on the PHx plug-in to explore further.

As you can see from the next screenshot, a plug-in is similar to a snippet in that it has a plug-in name and PHP code.

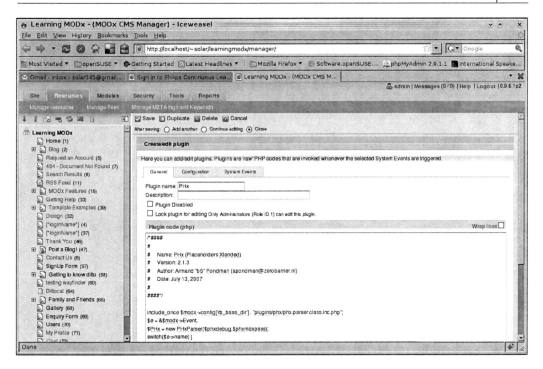

You will also be able to see two other tabs—**Configuration** and **System Events**. Let us look into each of these tabs.

Configuration

The configuration screen (as shown next) has the category selection boxes for the plug-in just like any other resource in MODx. There is also an option called **Import module shared properties**, which we will discuss in the next section on modules. Using the Plugin Configuration text area, you can pass parameters to the plug-in. There is a specific syntax to do so. All values have to be passed as a `key : value` pair separated by a comma. There are five parts to a configuration parameter—the parameter name, its label, the data type, optional values, and a default value. Each parameter must begin with `&`. The parameter values are separated by a `;`.

The following example is taken from the **TinyMCE** plug-in:

```
&entity_encoding=Entity Encoding;list;named,numeric,raw;raw
```

This defines a configuration variable named `entity_encoding`. The label used when displaying the parameter editing form will be **Entity Encoding**. Its type is a `list`, with three options—`named`, `numeric`, and `raw`. The default value is `raw`.

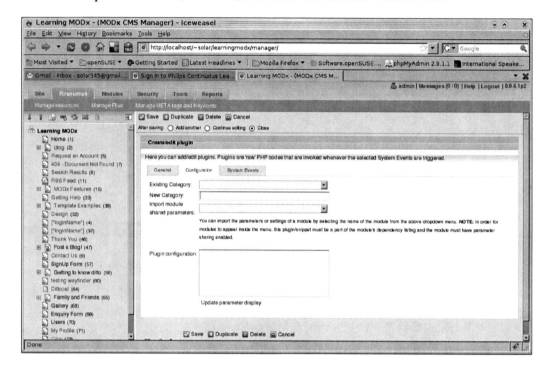

System events

In this screen (shown opposite), you will see a list of events. When the checkbox next to any event is selected, the plug-in will get executed when that event happens. For example, we are viewing the PHx plug-in and, as we can see, the checkbox next to **onParseDocument** is selected. This will make MODx execute the PHP code for the PHx snippet just before parsing the document.

If you take a moment now to think about how PHx works, you will understand the whole concept better. MODx fetches a document and, just before parsing, executes the PHx plug-in. The code in the PHx plug-in is written to search and replace the PHx notations with their corresponding result. In the subsection on creating plug-ins, we will discuss how to take a document, process it, and send it back to MODx as output.

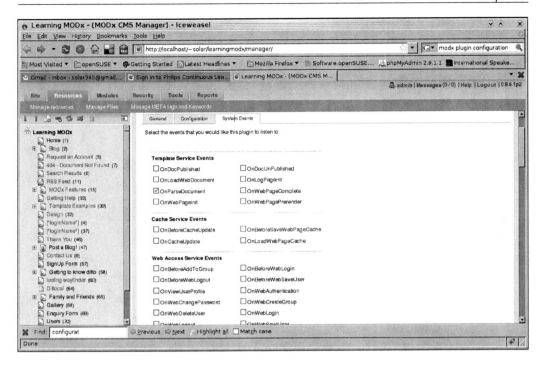

Exploring other plug-ins

Now is a good time to go through the other plug-ins and notice their triggering events. It will help your understanding to think why the **QuickEdit** plug-in is triggered by the **OnWebPagePrerender** event and so on.

Using custom plug-ins

In this section, we will download a plug-in called `Codeprettify` and learn how to use it. The following steps describe how to do this:

1. Download the plug-in from `http://MODxcms.com/CodePrettify-1650.html` and extract it.

2. Click on **New plugin** from **Resources | Manage Resources | Plugins**.

3. Fill in the following details:

Field Name	Field Value
Plugin name	Code Prettify
Plugin code	Copy and paste the code from `plugin.codeprettify.tpl`
Configuration | Category	Learning Modx
System Events	OnLoadWebDocument: Checked

4. Click on **Save.**

5. Copy the `codeprettify` directory that you have extracted to the `assets/plugins` directory.

Note that it doesn't matter what name you give the plug-in, as you will not be invoking it by any call; rather it gets invoked on the selected events automatically. As stated for all the elements, a category is just used to allow the developer to group the elements visually and doesn't affect the functionality.

If you notice the selected **System Events**, the trigger is **OnLoadWebDocument**. You may wonder why it is not **OnWebPagePrerender**. This is because this plug-in inserts JavaScript, and it is better to do so before the document is generated.

Now let's go ahead and test the plug-in.

Create a document with the following details:

Field Name	Field Value
Title	Testing Plugin
Uses Template	Learning Modx default template
Document content	echo "This code is pretty printed by the new plugin";

Now a preview of the document will look like the following:

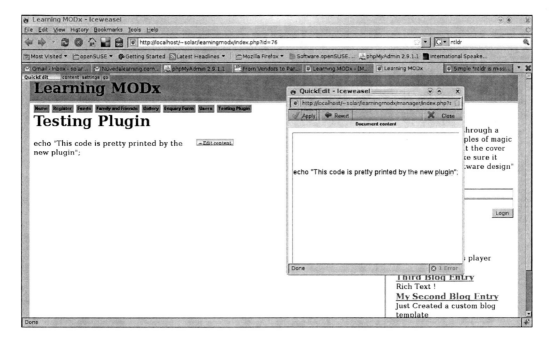

As you can see, there is no visible difference; this is because this plug-in requires all the code that has to be prettified inserted within:

```
<pre class="prettyprint"> </pre>
```

So, to test pretty printing, change the contents of the document to the following:

```
<pre class="prettyprint">
echo "This code is pretty printed by the new plugin";
</pre>
```

Now the preview will look like the following:

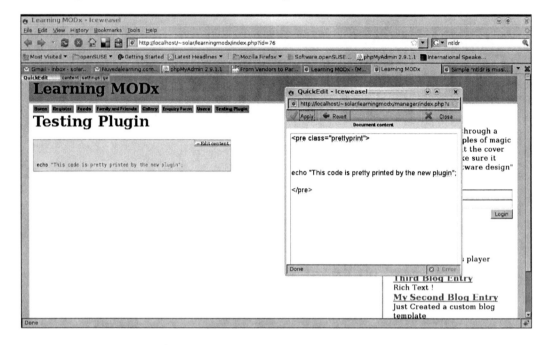

Learning about the plug-in

When using the previous plug-in, there were a few details that we couldn't have intuitively known. For instance, we couldn't have known which tags are to be used in the document and which events have to be enabled. So it is important that for every plug-in that you want to use, you read the associated document. Many plug-ins come with a separate document, some have the details in the download page. But some plug-ins have the details of how to use the plug-in as comments within the file that contains the plug-in code. In our last example, we can get the details from the plug-in code.

As you will be able to see if you open the `plugin.codeprettify.tpl` file, the top section contains the following:

```
/*
 * CodePrettify *
 *
 * DESCRIPTION: Allows syntax highlighting of code blocks, using the
 * google-code-prettify javascript
 *
 * HISTORY:
 * version 0.5 (2007-09-08): by Daniele "MadMage" Calisi
```

```
 *
 * NOTES: google-code-prettify can be downloaded from Google Code
website (http://code.google.com/p/google-code-prettify/)
 * and is under the Apache 2.0 license
      (http://www.apache.org/licenses)
 *
 * INSTRUCTIONS:
 * - extract the content of the zip archive in
                    assets/plugins/codeprettify
 * - create a new MODx plugin using the code of this file
 * - select "OnLoadWebDocument" as the System Event that will trigger
                                                        this plugin
 * - all source code in the webpage enclosed in <code
                    class="prettyprint">...</code>
 *   or in <pre class="prettyprint">...</pre> will be automatically
                                                        prettified.
 * - you can optionally put some css in assets/plugins/codeprettify/
prettify-custom.css file
 */
```

One key skill that is very important in a community-driven platform, like MODx, is to be able to search and read through documentation. This may, in many cases, help you to avoid having to reinvent the wheel, and help to get you a quicker solution for something that is challenging your mental abilities.

Creating plug-ins

To create a plug-in, you have to just remember this one rule: the plug in code tells MODx what has to get executed for which event. MODx passes the event details to the plug-in along with the MODx resource that we examined in the last chapter. $MODx->Event holds the details of the event. $MODx->Event->name gives you the name of the event. So, the plug-in code will have to check the name of the triggered event and execute the appropriate code. This can easily be done with a switch statement. Hence, the structure of code specific to the events in a plug-in would look like this:

```
$e = & $MODx->Event;
switch ($e->name) {
   case "eventname1" :
                        Code for eventname1
                        break;
   case "eventname2"   :
                        Code for eventname2
                        break;
   default             :
                        return;
                        break;
```

Now is a good time to look into the source code of the previous plug-in, as you will be able to understand exactly how the plug-in works the way it does. If you want to use the external files from your plug-in, then the convention is to place these files in a separate folder within the `assets/plugins` directory. The following is the code from the plug-in that we just used:

```
switch ($MODx->Event->name) {
    case "OnLoadWebDocument":
        $MODx->regClientCSS('assets/plugins/
                codeprettify/prettify.css');
        $MODx->regClientCSS('assets/plugins/codeprettify/prettify-
                                            custom.css');
        $MODx->regClientStartupScript('manager/media/script/mootools/
                                            mootools.js');
        $MODx->regClientStartupScript('assets/plugins/codeprettify/
                                            prettify.js');
        $jspp = '<script type="text/javascript">';
        $jspp .= 'window.addEvent("domready", prettyPrint);';
        $jspp .= '</script>';
        $MODx->regClientStartupScript($jspp);
        break;
    default:   // stop here
        return;
        break;
}
```

Similar to what you have just learned, the plug-in uses a `switch` case to check for the event along with the `$MODx->Event->name` API. We can see that it executes a portion of the code for only the `OnLoadWebDocument` event, and for any other event, it just returns without changing anything.

Let us now examine what the portion of code that gets executed for the event does. The code uses a few API functions that we haven't yet discussed. The following table explains these APIs.

Field Name	Field Value
`$MODx->regClientCSS`	This API can be used to load a CSS at the beginning of the page. The CSS loaded using this function will be inserted within the `<head></head>` tag. The function takes one argument, which is the name of the CSS file, or the CSS content itself.
`regClientStartupScript`	Similar to the previous API, but in this case loads a JavaScript file within the `<head></head>` tag instead of the CSS.

As you can see, the discussed plug-in does two things;

1. Inserts the `<style .... />` tag for CSS.
2. Inserts the `<script ...></script>` tag for JavaScript.

This plug-in, as it says in the comments, is using a JavaScript from the Google code that already does the pretty printing. The functionality of this plug-in is to just ensure that the JavaScript code and the CSS are loaded for every document irrespective of the template used. As you may realize, plug-ins affect the system-wide behavior for the selected events.

Event-triggering snippets

It is possible to trigger events from your snippets to get a plug-in to do something.

The API to do this is `$MODx->invokeEvent`. `invokeEvent` takes two parameters, the name of the event and the parameters to be passed. For example:

```
$MODx->invokeEvent("OnBeforeWebLogin", $parameters);
```

This API is generally not recommended for usage because it is intended for the core code. Anyways, if you are curious and want to try out the API, going through the code of the `WebloginPE` snippet can be a good start.

Modules

In this section, we will learn how to use modules and how a module works.

Modules are code that can be executed only from the Manager interface. Modules are useful for the following two purposes.

1. Adding functionality to the Manger interface.
   - An example of this kind of functionality is the DOC Manager module, which is an optional component during the MODx installation. This module allows the Manager to perform bulk actions on documents.
2. Creating tables that the snippets can use.
   - Snippets and plug-ins may need to store data in the database. Modules can facilitate this by creating these tables for the snippets or plug-ins. Also, it can be used for creating an interface for the Manager to add data that gets stored in the database that snippets or plug-ins can use. In this section, we will look into a module and plug-in pair to demonstrate this functionality.

Using modules

In this section, we will install a module called **Autolink**. This module provides the Manager with an interface to create the keywords that the accompanying snippet can use. The following are the steps to use the module:

Creating a module

1. Download the module and the plug-in package from `http://MODxcms.com/Autolink-507.html` and extract it.

2. Click on **New Module** from **Modules | Manage Modules.**

3. Fill in the following details:

Field Name	Field Value
Module name	Autolink
Module code	Code from `autolink_module.txt`
Category	Learning MODx

4. Click on **Save.**

Executing a module

Once you have created a module, you will have to manually execute it from the Manager interface. The following steps will show you how:

1. You will see the module listed with the other modules.

2. Next to the module, there is a small icon. Clicking on the icon opens a context menu.

3. Click on **Run module** from the Context menu.

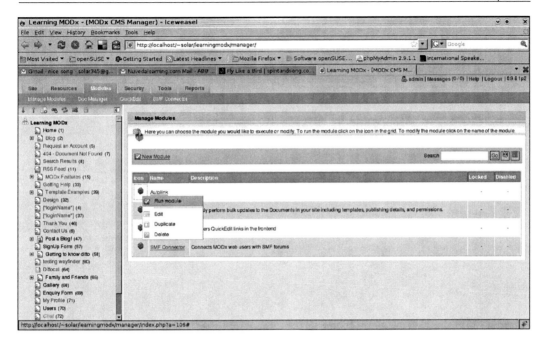

4. Now you will notice a new link next to the **SMF Connector** at the top, after refreshing the page.

Module's Manager interface

The execution of the module has provided us with a page in the Manager interface where we can use its functionalities. The **Autolink** module allows us to define the keywords that will be used by the plug-in. The plug-in replaces the keywords with an appropriate link. Let us, for now, just add one keyword—**MODx**—with the value **google**. This should allow the plug-in to create a link that searches for "MODx" in Google.

1. Click on **Add Keywords** in **Modules | Manage Modules | Autolink**.
2. Fill in the following details:

Field Name	Field Value
Keyword	MODx
Value	google
Title	Google MODx

3. Click on **Add Keywords** at the bottom of the form.

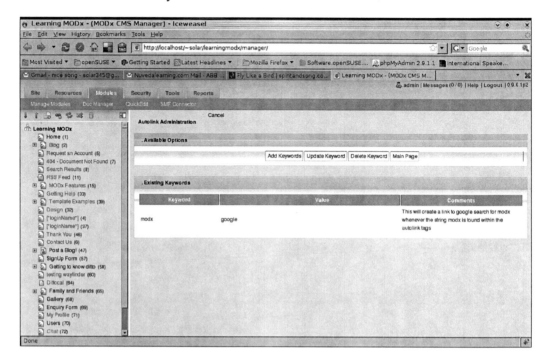

Dependent plug-ins

Now that we have installed the module that allows the creation of keywords from the Manager interface, let us create the accompanying plug-in that will convert the keywords to links in a document.

1. Click on **New plugin** from **Resources | Manage resources | Plugins**.

2. Fill in the following data:

Field Name	Field Value
Plugin name	Autolink
Plugin code	Code from `autolink_plugin_v2.txt`
Configuration	Category	`Learning MODx`
System Events	OnWebPagePrerender: checked

3. Click on **Save**.

Let us test the combined functionality of the module and the plug-in by creating a document with the following contents:

Field Name	Field Value
Title	Testing Modules
Uses template	`Learning MODx default template`

Document content	`<autolink>`
	`MODx`
	`</autolink>`

Now preview the above document and it will look like the following:

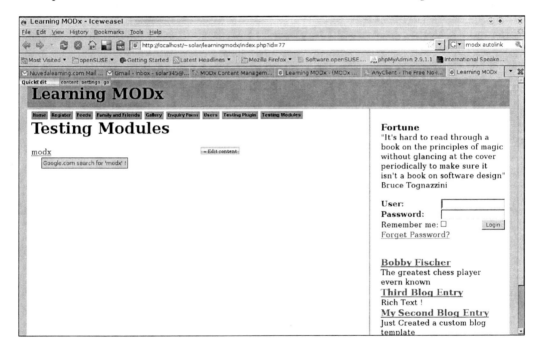

If you notice, the keyword has been changed to a link that is a Google search for "MODx". This is shown in the status bar of the browser at the bottom, and the title has been used for the tooltip. So, the plug-in has got these values from what we inserted into the Modules page.

Remember that this section teaches you how to use modules and not Autolink. You must also remember that there is no need to have a relation between the module name and the plug-in name. The plug-in merely reads the values from the database using the regular MODx db API that we discussed earlier.

```
Ex: $rs = $MODx->db->select('*', $autolinkTable);
```

Unlike snippets and plug-ins, we will not learn how to create modules, as to make efficient modules, you must first understand certain design patterns.

Learning to use custom modules

Since the installation of modules and plug-ins that come as a package involves multiple steps, it can be a little confusing in the beginning. It will be very easy to understand if you keep in mind a few points. Modules are used for providing some functionality in the Manager interface, and for sharing the results of such interaction, like data collected, with plug-ins and snippets.

Summary

In this chapter, we have learned about plug-ins and modules

- The differences between plug-ins and modules:
  - Snippets are executed when they are explicitly called either in a document, template, or from another snippet.
  - Plug-ins are executed on the trigger of events with which they are associated. This allows the plug-in code to be executed just before the document rendering, user registration, and so on, as needed.
  - Modules are executed only from within the Manager. They are used for creating the tables that dependent plug-ins or snippets may want to use. Modules can also provide the values for plug-in and snippet parameters.
- You have also learned how to use plug-ins and how to use customize plug-ins.
- You have also learned how to create new plug-ins, and we analyzed the code of the prettify code plug-in that we used.
- You have also learned how to use modules by using the Autolink module and the plug-in package with an example document.

Index

M

Thank you for buying
MODx Web Development

Packt Open Source Project Royalties

When we sell a book written on an Open Source project, we pay a royalty directly to that project. Therefore by purchasing MODx Web Development, Packt will have given some of the money received to the MODx Project.

In the long term, we see ourselves and you—customers and readers of our books—as part of the Open Source ecosystem, providing sustainable revenue for the projects we publish on. Our aim at Packt is to establish publishing royalties as an essential part of the service and support a business model that sustains Open Source.

If you're working with an Open Source project that you would like us to publish on, and subsequently pay royalties to, please get in touch with us.

Writing for Packt

We welcome all inquiries from people who are interested in authoring. Book proposals should be sent to authors@packtpub.com. If your book idea is still at an early stage and you would like to discuss it first before writing a formal book proposal, contact us; one of our commissioning editors will get in touch with you.

We're not just looking for published authors; if you have strong technical skills but no writing experience, our experienced editors can help you develop a writing career, or simply get some additional reward for your expertise.

About Packt Publishing

Packt, pronounced 'packed', published its first book "Mastering phpMyAdmin for Effective MySQL Management" in April 2004 and subsequently continued to specialize in publishing highly focused books on specific technologies and solutions.

Our books and publications share the experiences of your fellow IT professionals in adapting and customizing today's systems, applications, and frameworks. Our solution-based books give you the knowledge and power to customize the software and technologies you're using to get the job done. Packt books are more specific and less general than the IT books you have seen in the past. Our unique business model allows us to bring you more focused information, giving you more of what you need to know, and less of what you don't.

Packt is a modern, yet unique publishing company, which focuses on producing quality, cutting-edge books for communities of developers, administrators, and newbies alike. For more information, please visit our website: www.PacktPub.com.

PUBLISHING

Building Websites with
Joomla! 1.5

ISBN: 978-1-847195-30-2   Paperback: 363 pages

The best-selling Joomla! tutorial guide updated for
the latest 1.5 release

1. Learn Joomla! 1.5 features

2. Install and customize Joomla! 1.5

3. Configure Joomla! administration

4. Create your own Joomla! templates

5. Extend Joomla! with new components,
   modules, and plug-ins

Building Powerful and Robust
Websites with Drupal 6

ISBN: 978-1-847192-97-4   Paperback: 362 pages

Build your own professional blog, forum, portal or
community website with Drupal 6

1. Set up, configure, and deploy Drupal 6

2. Harness Drupal's world-class Content
   Management System

3. Design and implement your website's look
   and feel

4. Easily add exciting and powerful features

5. Promote, manage, and maintain your
   live website

Please check **www.PacktPub.com** for information on our titles

Printed in the United States
214202BV00002B/11/P

9 781847 194909